Exploring Dimensional
Quilt Art

Stitch, Fold, Embellish

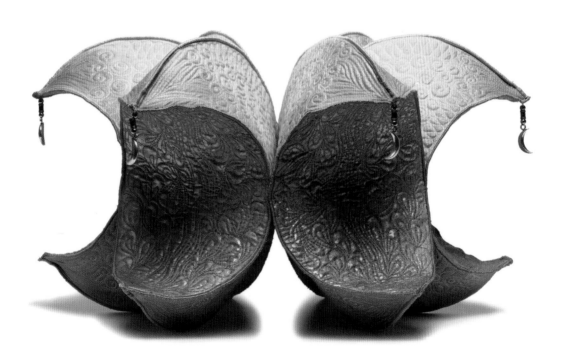

C. June Barnes

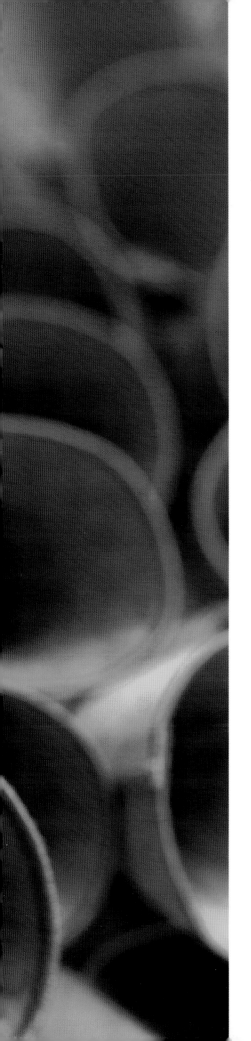

Exploring
Dimensional
Quilt Art

Stitch, Fold, Embellish

C. June Barnes

INTERWEAVE.
interweave.com

Acknowledgments

What would I do without the tolerance and support of my family? Thank you!

A special thanks to those wonderful friends who have trawled through my diagrams and explanations to see if they make sense! Their advice has been invaluable.

I dedicate this book to all those who are prepared to work outside their comfort zone; who like pushing the boundaries and who ask "What if...?"

Cover image (shown on page 111), *Empty Vessel,* by Inger Milburn.

First published in the United States in 2012 by
Interweave
201 East Fourth Street
Loveland, CO 80537
www.interweave.com

Copyright © Batsford, 2012
Text © C. June Barnes, 2012

The moral rights of the author have been asserted.

Reproduction by Rival Colour Ltd, UK
Printed by 1010 Printing International Ltd, China

Library of Congress Cataloging-in-Publication Data
Barnes, C. J. (C. June)
  Exploring dimensional quilt art : stitch, fold, embellish / C. June Barnes.
    pages cm
  Includes bibliographical references and index.
  ISBN 978-1-59668-588-8 (pbk.)
1. Quilting. 2. Art quilts--Design. I. Title.
  TT835.B26655 2012
  746.46--dc23
                                        2011052799

ISBN-13: 978-1-59668-588-8

20 19 18 17 16 15 14 13 12
10 9 8 7 6 5 4 3 2 1

Contents

Introduction

We are surrounded by dimension. Everything we see has dimension. Despite this, the preference in quiltmaking is to create flat artwork. In this book I explore the endless possibilities for creating dimensional quilt art; adding depth, shape, structure, and form to what is traditionally a two-dimensional craft. Wearables, such as cushions, bags, and hats are not within the scope of this book as these are extensively explored in many other publications. The ideas presented here could be used to enhance such items, however. This book concentrates on form, not function. Some of the exercises offer opportunities to create useful items, but all can lead to more artistic interpretations as seen in the examples chosen.

Visual dimension or an illusion of dimension (where a single plane appears to have dimension), can be achieved through the clever use of light and dark. The most common geometric example of such an illusion is "baby blocks" (see below), but there are many other designs and patterns that achieve this effect through the use of contrast. Many quilters in this book, inspired by artists such as Vasarely and Escher, have used this aspect in their design choices.

Physical or spatial dimension is the measurable extent (length, breadth, height) of an object or space. The dimension is defined as the minimum number of coordinates needed to specify each point within a shape or space. So a line has a dimension of one, as only one coordinate is needed to specify a point on it.

A plane or surface of a sphere has a dimension of two because two coordinates are needed to specify a point on it. For example, to locate a point on a sphere (as on the earth) two coordinates are needed – the latitude and longitude. The *inside* of a sphere, however, is three-dimensional because three coordinates are needed to locate a point within it. Beyond the spatial dimension of an object we can consider other broader dimensions such as movement, light, sound, smell, and even time. These offer some interesting areas for further exploration!

Although the norm is to produce two-dimensional quilt art, many artists have been working with dimension and some of these artists are introduced to you with examples of their work in the final section of this book. I hope that you will enjoy exploring this area of quiltmaking with me through this book, and that you will be inspired to have a go yourself.

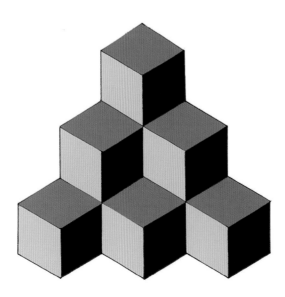

Left:
Baby blocks — a traditional pattern that creates the illusion of three dimensions.

Right:
Squaring Up (C. June Barnes)
24" x 39" (60 x 100cm)
This award-winning quilt incorporates many three-dimensional techniques, including shrinkage (see page 18).

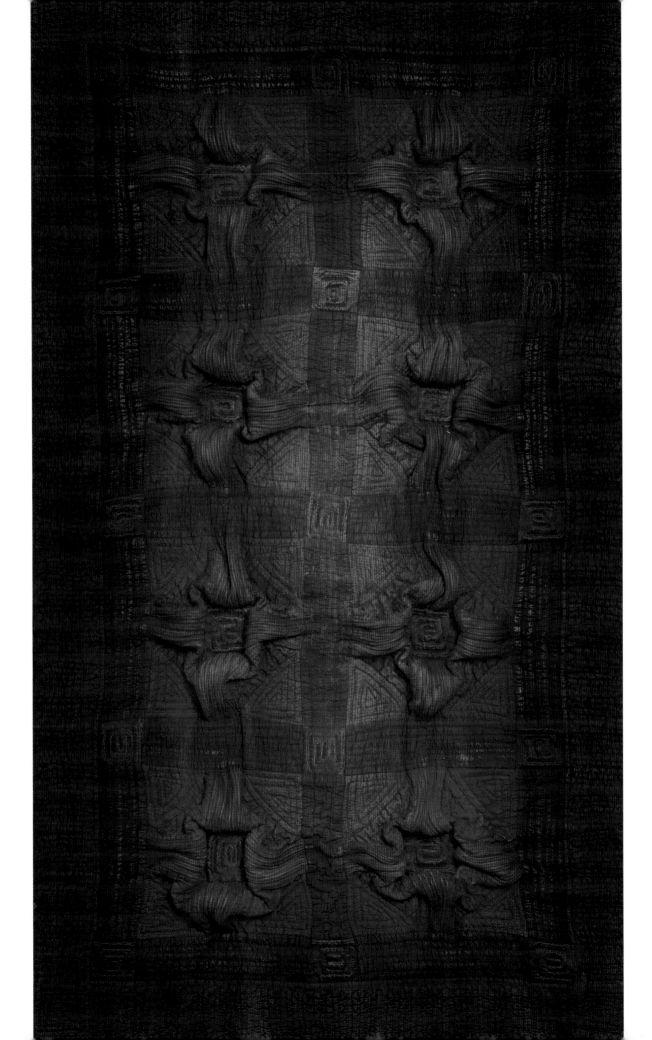

Inspiration

The question always asked is "How does one come up with original ideas?"

The trouble is that there are very few! Most of what is produced has been inspired by other designs, adapting what others have used to create something using our own preferred medium. Although we may not realize it, something we make will have taken root from a seed planted perhaps many years ago. This was the case with the folded pieces, particularly *Split Down the Middle* (see page 26). When I showed these to a friend she said that she had seen something similar before. After further investigation and rummaging through boxes of cuttings I found that years ago we had both seen an article by Penny Burnfield who had made very similar structures using paper. It seems that we all store information subconsciously and access it later without realizing where it came from!

Our surroundings are filled with shapes, objects, and structures – both man-made and natural. We can find a wealth of ideas by looking at the shapes of what we see around us and considering how they could be translated into stitched projects. Don't be put off by scale – something as large as the Gherkin (30 St Mary Axe in London) can be the inspiration for a more manageably sized project. At the other end of the scale the use of micro-photography reveals the incredible world of plants, enabling us to see the molecular structure of seeds, pollen, and fruit in glorious detail.

A camera and notebook are essential items to have on hand when it comes to recording ideas as you go about your daily business. You never know when you will see something that is inspirational. Look at everyday objects such as toys, kitchen equipment, buildings, ornaments, and packaging. Everything has a shape of some sort or another and can often be interpreted or adapted to use as a starting point for a dimensional piece of artwork. Nature is also a rich source of inspiration – look at how leaves are arranged, how flowers are constructed, and how seedpods are shaped.

Three of the creations featured in this book have their roots in childhood things. Some of the folded pieces are based on Scoubidou weaving I did as a child; *Fortunity* (see page 29) is a landscape made up of "fortune teller" origami folded game we played as children. There is also great value in revisiting ideas that have already been examined. *Bottle Mania!* (see pages 92–93) is a progression in my bottle enthusiasm. Having previously explored them in two and two-and-a-half dimensions, making three-dimensional models seemed like the obvious next step.

Below:
A camera and notebook are essential items to have on hand for recording ideas. You never know when you will see something inspirational, from natural formations such as pebbles or ripples in sand to architectural features.

Keep your eyes open while watching films; look at the stage sets – especially in fantasy films – a rich source of new ideas. The idea for *Magic Circles* (page 40) came from the movie *Avatar*.

I find looking at the work of sculptors, jewelery makers, basket makers, and ceramicists very stimulating. Andy Goldsworthy, Louise Hibbert, Claire Palastanga, Jodie Hatcher, and Peter Randall-Page are particularly inspirational. Surfing the internet for images, using words such as *sculpture*, *organic*, *structures*, or *forms* will produce a wealth of examples.

All things start from just one idea. It doesn't matter where the idea comes from – all that matters is that you explore it, develop it, and make use of it by creating something of your own. Some ideas may lie dormant for a long time before you wake up one morning and think "What if I take that idea and...?"

Ask the What if...? question often. For me it is still the most productive tool. My most exciting discoveries come from the process of working; as I stitch my way through a project new ideas spring to mind as a result of asking this question. You need to make a note of the answers as and when they occur to you – it is often very difficult to grasp or remember an idea that came to you at three in the morning!

Be inquisitive. Wonder how and why something was achieved. The answer you come up with may not be the one that was behind the creation you see, but it will more than likely be a useful one, and one that may lead you to do something different. It may be that you apply it to an idea that has been waiting in the wings of your mind for just such a solution.

Challenges can be another way to come up with a new idea. I have for many years belonged to an exhibiting group, Hanging Together. We introduced a challenge to exhibit an item that was outside the box, something that was not necessarily displayed on the wall and which was inspired by a phrase or tag. This has meant that over the years I have flirted with artworks that have explored dimension for these challenges. These have been inspired by subjects such as Looking Through, Empty Vessels, and Openings. Examples of some items made by Inger Milburn, Sandra Grusd, and myself as a result of these challenges are shown in this book. Openings was the word that inspired Sandra's *Colourdance* (see page 52) and Inger Milburn produced the wonderful *Looking Through* (see page 39). Other topics included Long and Thin, Up in the Air, and Off the Wall. You could try similar phrases to generate ideas.

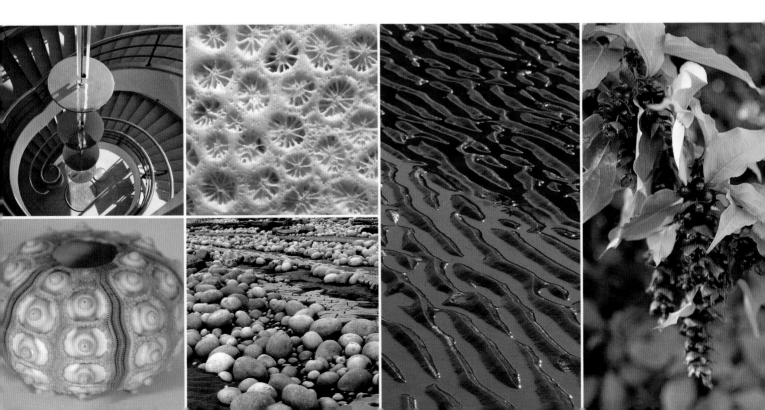

Verb command prompts are useful tools that work in a similar way.
Sometimes we just need a little assistance to help find a new and innovative
way to use an idea or starting point we may have, which needs just that little
spark to generate a new and interesting design. Not all the phrases in the
following table will be appropriate, but one just may work its magic for you.

VERB COMMAND PROMPTS

Make it bigger	Make it smaller	Make it tiny
Make it BIG	Elongate it	Simplify it
Make it round	Make it square	Make it longer
Make it shorter	Make it heavier	Make it lighter
Make it sparkle	Make it light up	Enclose it
Fill it up	Empty it	Coil it
Twist it	Combine it	Make it glow
Open it	Turn it upside down	Lay it on its side
Stretch it	Shrink it	Change its colour
Refine it	Eliminate parts of it	Distort it
Use repetition	Make it two- or three-dimensional	Change the shape
Change a part of it	Make it part of a set	Mechanize it
Electrify it	Make it move	Reverse it
Make it look like something else	Rotate it	Make it part of something else
Repeat it	Turn it inside out	Give it texture
Make it revolve	Make it stronger	Make it fragile
Make it durable	Use symbolism	Be unrealistic
Contain it	Make it cooler	Make it hotter
Add ingredients	Twist it	Make it transparent
Make it opaque	Glamorize it	Use another material
Add human interest	Make it compact	Miniaturize it
Make it collapsible	Go to extremes	Summarize it
Make it shine	Make it grow	Split it
Make it darker	Exaggerate it	Subtract it
Add it	Divide it	Use the obvious
Lower it	Raise it	Isolate it
Condense it	Bend it	Match it
Suspend it	Make it stand upright	Make it lie flat
Concentrate it	Make it symmetrical	Make it asymmetrical
Sharpen it	Depress it	Spread it out
Solidify it	Liquify it	Soften it
Harden it	Make it narrow	Make it wider
Make it funny or silly	Make it fly	Squash it
Flatten it	Fold it	Unfold it
Extend it	Make it uncomfortable	Use a different texture
Make it slapstick	Extrude it	

Using this Book

To add dimension to an object we need to increase the physical measurement of its depth. A single plane has no depth – only length and width or breadth.

This book concentrates on spatial dimension using the medium of quilted, stitched layers. The two qualifying requirements are that the object be constructed of a stitched or quilted surface, comprising a minimum of two layers, and that the depth of the work should exceed that achieved by the conventional quilt sandwich.

Spatial dimension is achieved when an object occupies space in three directions – height, width, and depth. In some instances the depth of a piece can be minimal. It could be argued that the very nature of quilted layers is three-dimensional as depth is achieved through the layering of fabric and batting – the depth of the work is greater than a single plane. However, for the purpose of this book a depth of more than the usual two or three layers is required to qualify the work as being three-dimensional – concentrating on increasing the depth of the work to be greater than that achieved through assembling the usual two or three layers.

Spatial dimension can be achieved in the following ways:

- Manipulating the surface of the quilted plane to achieve depth.
- Adding to the surface to increase the depth.
- Manipulating the quilted plane or layers through folding, wrapping, curling and so on to either construct a shape or create depth.
- Constructing objects through various means, the outer layer being a quilted surface (although some of the exercises use only bonded layers to demonstrate a process).

Some of the basic structures in this book are utilitarian and have very little connection to quilt art, but these can be used to produce more artistic creations; playing with the dimensions and assembling multiple units of a structure are just two ways to use the structures explored. In order to translate ideas into beautiful creations you need tools, which this book aims to provide.

At first glance it may seem that what follows is a book on maths! However, at the core of most structures displaying dimension is a physical construction, and this aspect is an essential part of the creative process. Converting ideas into physical, three-dimensional installations involves working out how the structure will be constructed and supported.

Translating a three-dimensional idea into a textile creation requires a pattern, and making that pattern to the size you want involves some basic geometry. This means that, out of necessity, the book does get to be quite technical.

The underlying construction involved in creating any inspirational and innovative art exhibit is usually very practical and not at all glamorous. Perhaps we need to be reminded that behind any finished work lies a tremendous amount of research and thought, and that results don't always come easily. This book endeavours to show solutions to a number of problems, and provide practical methods of making shapes, building structures and assembling modules.

I hope that by showing ways of constructing a range of shapes I am providing you with a useful tool kit for exploring dimension in quilt art works.

Below:
Kissed By a Rose, detail
(C. June Barnes).
Here, the inherent texture of a quilt is pushed to greater depth using shrinkage (see pages 18–21).

Getting Started

The following list includes items that I have found useful in the construction of three-dimensional quilt art. They are offered for your consideration but many other suitable products are available. The usual sewing equipment and materials are not listed here.

- Cotton batting, both stabilized and unstabilized.
- Wool-viscose felt or other wool-based product that shrinks.
- Stuffing or filling, such as polyester toy filling, plastic pellet beads, or vermiculite (insulation and packaging material).
- Lightweight interfacing: useful for trapping objects under the top layer when working with shrinkage.
- Fusible web: both normal and extra-strong weights. The heavier weight is useful for bonding heavier fabrics, and in some instances will add just enough stability to two layers to make them more manageable when used in three-dimensional structures. The lightweight web is necessary for working with fine fabrics such as silk.
- Interfacings or linings such as:
  - buckram and hessian buckram
  - Fast2Fuse interfacing, which is fusible on both sides
  - Pellon Peltex, available as single- or double-side adhesive interfacing
  - Laminating sheets (stiff, transparent sheets, which are ironed on to fabric – including silks – to protect and reinforce; an excellent stabilizer.
  - Timtex (equivalent to Pellon Peltex #70 sew-in firm), firm, flexible interfacing.
- Fabric stiffeners, available in liquid or spray form.
- Selection of wires in various weights and thicknesses.
- Various rods and tubes, such as wooden dowels, metal or aluminium and acrylic rods and tubes.
- Foam shapes, which can be cut at specialist shops.
- Firm card or foam board.
- Acrylic sheets.
- Scoubidou laces.
- Monofilament cord, such as used in garden strimmers.
- Boning products.
- Brim wire, as used by milliners.
- Cable ties.
- Eyelets.
- Washers, rubber and metal.
- Recycled products such as:
  - package strapping
  - plastic sheets as used for packaging or covers of folders and files
  - old buttons
  - old metal zippers.

Equipment

- A handyman or woman is useful!
- Glue gun.
- Staple gun.
- Clover mini iron, useful for small fusing jobs.
- Hot-air craft tool, for use with some paint products.
- Bulldog clips, all sizes, but tiny ones are useful for holding sections in place while assembling some items.
- Hemostat clamps or forceps are very useful. They help with turning shapes after stitching and are also invaluable when taking pins out while stitching fiddly seams.
- Craft knife and other cutting tools such as a hacksaw.
- Ruler with accurate, clear markings.
- Geometric drawing tools – protractor, set square and compasses.
- Large sheets of paper, such as from a flipchart.
- Bradawl or awl, a hand tool with a pointed metal end, very useful for making holes.
- Hammer.
- Drill and drill bits.

Sewing Techniques

The projects and exercises presented assume a basic sewing knowledge and are well within a wide range of ability levels. No specific stitching instruction is given, but the following notes are offered as guidance. Please also refer to the glossary for an explanation of some words and terms used in the text. The work in this book uses machine stitching and quilting, but handstitching techniques could be used, if preferred.

Below:
Magic Circles, detail
(C. June Barnes).
Detail of the quilted surface of one of three spirals that form *Magic Circles* (see page 40).

General assembly notes for three-dimensional structures

It is easiest first to draw the pattern shapes on to a lightweight interfacing or cotton fabric, leaving space between them to add seam allowances. Choose a thin batting or felt, especially for small items. A batting that has no stabilizer is best as it allows the pieces to "give" more, contributing to more accurate results. Place the marked interfacing on to the underside of the felt or batting to be used and add the chosen fabric on the other side. Firstly stitch around the shapes along the seam or stitching lines, working from the back of the sandwich, stitching through all layers. This serves as stay stitching (stabilizing the curves and so on) and also marks the shape so that it can be seen on the front. Next, quilt within the stitching lines of each piece from the front before cutting out and add an allowance for seams.

Registration marks on a pattern indicate which points on a seam must match and allow you to stitch curves accurately. Use as many pins as necessary when preparing tricky seams for stitching. Snip into curves to help ease seams – the sharper the curve the more snips needed. Stitch just inside the stay-stitching lines so that they will not be visible on the finished article. Leave an adequate opening for turning and filling. Stitching the seam twice adds the strength necessary to cope with the pressure of stuffing. Before turning, reduce the bulk of the seams by cutting away the batting in the seam allowances. When firmly stuffed, close the opening with handstitching.

Treatment of edges

The edges of many of the pieces are over-sewn. My preference is to neaten edges with satin stitch, a closely packed zigzag stitch about 3mm wide. Most edges are stitched twice and some more, depending on how thick the layers are. I always start with one row of stitches that are not as closely packed, followed by a second with a shorter stitch length – equivalent to that used for a buttonhole. Using a heavier-weight thread (see thread weight in the Glossary, see page 126) also helps. The aim is to avoid fluffy edges with none of the white batting showing through. Giving the fabric a good trim prior to over-sewing, especially on bias edges, helps minimize a messy finish. In extreme cases I resort to the use of permanent markers to hide any white showing through.

It is, of course, quite acceptable to use raw edges or open zigzag stitch if the project calls for it. Edges can also be bound as in *Upper Reaches* (see page 103). The folded *Scoubidous* on pages 25–27 have a single zigzag edge.

Stitch

Although I love quilting and still get tremendous pleasure from doing it, this book doesn't go into the topic in detail. Suffice to say that surface stitch is the icing on the cake and in my view pieces seem to be unfinished without it. While quilting is the main stitch used, all surfaces lend themselves to embroidery techniques and further embellishment.

Note: Nothing beats good habits when stitching:
- Don't rush, take your time and enjoy the process!
- Press often.
- Use pins to hold things in place – worth the time taken. I would rather take a bit more time at the assembling stage than overuse my seam ripper.

Embellishment

Often embellishment makes the difference between a successful project and one that has that extra wow factor. If it isn't something that you automatically do or even think about then I urge you to experiment with some of the products available. Take advantage of the demonstrations at exhibitions; ask the people selling products what various paints and products can be used for; research products online, or take a course. Play!

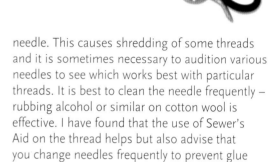

Threads

Consider threads other than the popular ones. Three-dimensional items are usually decorative and are not going to be subjected to a lot of wear and tear. This means that you can afford to use more fragile threads for decorative stitching. Try using rayon threads for quilting and think about using thicker threads. If these are too thick to use through the sewing-machine needle, try them in the bobbin and quilt from the wrong side. Metallic threads are not as problematic to use as you might think. Brands such as YLI Fine Metallic, Superior Metallic, and Isamet Metallic are very easy to use. Metallica needles and, if necessary, some Sewer's Aid can help things along. The same applies to handstitching – think of alternatives to the threads you automatically reach for.

Because some of the layers stitched involve bonding there is a tendency for the glue in these products to collect on the sewing-machine needle. This causes shredding of some threads and it is sometimes necessary to audition various needles to see which works best with particular threads. It is best to clean the needle frequently – rubbing alcohol or similar on cotton wool is effective. I have found that the use of Sewer's Aid on the thread helps but also advise that you change needles frequently to prevent glue accumulating on the needle.

Beads and sequins

Embellishments of this nature can be very successful. The danger is to overdo things – you do not want to distract from the piece itself; you want to enhance it, drawing attention to certain aspects. Surprise is something I love in pieces, something that rewards closer examination.

Paints

There are so many products available that it would not be possible to list them all here. Suffice to say that they can really make a difference to your projects. My favourite products are Shiva Paintstiks and similar products such as Treasure Gold. These are rubbed on to the surface of the fabric, adding depth, color and ambience to an otherwise dull surface, bringing it to life and taking it to a level that is rich and glowing.

Embossing powders are also an exciting product to experiment with. These were used to add interest to the depths of the components of *Fortunity* (see page 28), something unexpected that isn't obvious until the viewer comes in for a closer look.

Above right:
Selection of eyelets. These can be both practical and decorative

Below:
Selection of paints. Markal Paintstiks are wonderfully versatile and a current favourite of mine, but there are many excellent products to choose from

Right:
Ring Around the Moon, detail
(C. June Barnes).
12" x 21" (30 x 55cm)
The beaded moon charms hanging
from the upper points of this piece
draw attention to the curves and
hint at the meaning of the piece.
See page 84 for the full piece.

Presentation

Broadly speaking, the quilted objects explored here will fall into the following two categories.

The first category is two-and-a-half dimensions: those that you cannot move around. Examples of these include:

- Wall panels where the surface has been manipulated to add depth;
- Wall panels where the plane has been manipulated to add depth;
- Wall panels where additions have been made to the surface to add depth;
- Wall panels that are modular structures constructed from a collection of dimensional units.

The second is three dimensions: those that you can move around. Examples include:

- Forms or structures presented on a plinth;
- Columns standing on the floor and growing upwards (stalagmitic);
- Structures hanging down from the ceiling (stalactitic).

Right:
Fence post stakes from a garden center. Turned upside down, these provide ideal supports for hollow tubes, which in turn support stalagmitic structures.

A structure can be built either by assembling parts or pieces, which are quilted/stitched layers, or by covering a shape with a surface of quilted/stitched layers. In both instances some form of support is necessary to present or display the item. How three-dimensional pieces are displayed can present challenges that sometimes result in interesting solutions from unlikely places – a visit to a garden center or builders' merchant might result in some unexpected purchases!

The various types of structure all present their own, often unique, requirements. For example, the interior of a hollow shape can be stuffed with polystyrene pellets, sand, or cushion/toy filling. The bottles in *Bottle Mania!* (see pages 92–93) called for filling to show off their shape, but at the same time needed weight to keep them stable. The ideal filler was plastic pellet beads (the type used for stuffing teddy bears), but the quantity required was too great, making the cost impractical. They would also have been too heavy – ideal as door stops though! Both polystyrene pellets and soft toy stuffing were considered as alternatives, but they would have been too light and unstable. In the end the bottles were filled with vermiculite, which is an insulation product used in the building trade, but which is also sold as a packaging material. It was ideal, as it can be stuffed and packed into the shapes, offering good support and a solidity without being too heavy or expensive. The geometrical shapes in *Rounding Up* (see page 67) and many of the D-Forms and other spheres were filled very satisfactorily with good old-fashioned toy filler (polyester stuffing). They did need a lot of it though!

Sometimes wire, boning, stiffener, or similar material is a more suitable means of support. Wire was used to support Inger Milburn's *Orange Bowl* (see page 110) and the "ears" on the modules making up Sandra Grusd's *Colourdance* (see page 52) have a fine wire stitched into the edges so that they can be re-shaped as required. *Empty Vessel* (see page 96) has an underlying wooden framework; while support for *Pure Fantasy: Bommyknocker* (see page 77) was achieved by backing each panel with laminating sheets. This proved to be sufficient for the unit to hold the desired shape, but another

option would have been to use milliner's brim wire in the seams and to attach the assembled unit to an acrylic tube in the center. Others, such as *Ring Around the Moon* (see page 84), rely on the tension of the stiffened sides to keep their shape. *Pure Fantasy: Dodecahedron* (see page 73) and *Pure Fantasy: D-Formity* (see page 98) also rely on rigid linings to support their shapes, although tension between the two parts is a contributing factor in *Pure Fantasy: D-Formity*. This is also the case for the individual units of *Upper Reaches* (see page 103). Collectively they rely on a central rod to keep them together.

Both *Aspirations* (see page 34) and *Ascension* (see page 57) are pieces that rise from the floor, similarly made up of individual units which needed supporting on central columns. Both have acrylic rods running through eyelets at the center of the units. O-rings or rubber washers were fitted snugly on to the rods below each disc to maintain the spaces between them, which stopped the displayed items falling in a heap at the bottom of the rod. *Aspirations* posed an extra problem in that the pieces were not rigid enough to support their own weight, and so laminating sheets were added to the center area of their undersides to stop them flopping or drooping.

Some pieces rely on gravity to reveal their character; *Inner Spin* (see page 46) and *Stretching a Point* (see page 47) are suspended from the ceiling, their weight stretching them downwards into their shape.

Solid foam shapes such as cubes, cones, and cylinders can be used as foundations for three-dimensional objects. Lee Buchanan's *Jewel Boxes* (see page 68) uses polystyrene cubes to support the outer layers. Making supports out of papier mâché is an option offering flexibility when conventional shapes are not suitable.

Once you start making three-dimensional items you will find that some things never reach the rubbish or recycling bins because they offer possibilities for this sort of work. I find that I even buy products for their packaging – certain snack foods for their tubes and a particular washing powder because of the plastic handle (fortunately the powder works well too). These were used in *Woven Tub* (see page 24). Old venetian blinds, various tubes, polystyrene and packaging are all

items I have stashed away somewhere "just in case".

Some projects stand on the floor (stalagmitic), extending up from the ground, but seldom can do so on their own. They can be supported by cardboard tubing, but they in themselves also need support. This is where ingenuity comes into play. Inger Milburn had a special stand made to support her *Looking Through* (see page 39) and *Zip Tree* (see page 111), but I found gardening equipment works very well – a fence post stake when turned upside down serves as a superb support for a hollow tube.

Stalactitic installations that hang are less problematic but need overhead hooks or beams to hang from. In a gallery situation this may mean that brackets need to be attached to the wall so that there is an extension sticking out for them to hang from. Some projects lend themselves to being revolved, and for this you can use disco mirror-ball motors.

Most three-dimensional creations present a challenge when it comes to presenting and staging. Some solutions are offered in this book.

Above:
Selection of acrylic, wooden and metal rods. These can all be used to support three-dimensional pieces.

Surfaces

Surface Manipulation

Surfaces can be manipulated to create exaggerated texture, adding dimension through increased depth. This can be achieved by padding or stuffing some areas of the design (Trapunto), or through the use of shrinkage, which was explored in my book *Stitching to Dye in Quilt Art* (see Recommended Reading, page 127). Further explorations have resulted in some new discoveries.

Using shrinkage

If materials that resist shrinkage are added to the underside of the top layer of a project, and that layer stitched on to a material such as a wool-viscose felt that would shrink when washed, then the presence of the materials that resist shrinkage would result in a distortion to the combined layers.

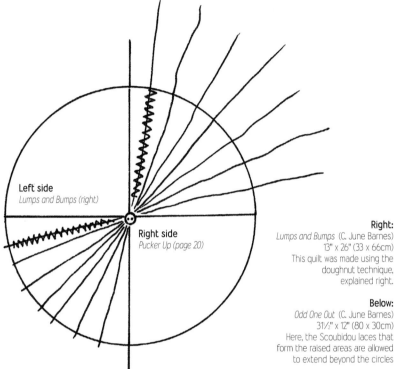

Left side
Lumps and Bumps (right)

Right side
Pucker Up (page 20)

Right:
Lumps and Bumps (C. June Barnes)
13" x 26" (33 x 66cm)
This quilt was made using the doughnut technique, explained right.

Below:
Odd One Out (C. June Barnes)
31½" x 12" (80 x 30cm)
Here, the Scoubidou laces that form the raised areas are allowed to extend beyond the circles

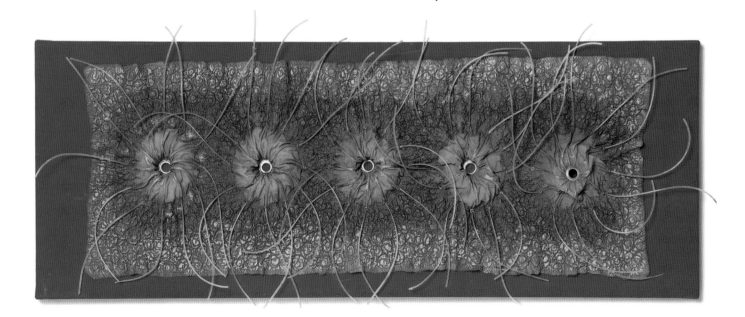

Doughnuts technique

This technique was used to make *Lumps and Bumps*. The piece was worked on white cotton sateen fabric and dyed after it was finished. It was embellished with Shiva Paintstiks.

Materials:
- Natural fiber fabric
- Wool-viscose felt
- Water-soluble thread
- Cotton thread
- Scoubidou (lanyard) wires/laces
- Small buttons

Method:
Refer to the "left side" section of the diagram shown opposite.

1 Using water-soluble pen, draw circles roughly twice the finished size on to the wrong side of the top fabric. Mark the circles' center.
2 Using water-soluble thread, stitch a small button to the center of the circle on the wrong side of each circle.
3 Using zigzag stitch and water-soluble thread, attach short lengths of the Scoubidou lace to the underside of each circle – each length radiating from the button at equal intervals. See the diagram shown opposite.
4 When all the buttons and laces have been stitched in place, pin a layer of wool-viscose felt to the underside, trapping the buttons and laces between the top layer and the felt.
   Note: For a more pronounced dome effect use a fine batting here instead of the wool-viscose felt.
5 Using cotton thread, free-machine stitch around the buttons and the laces, and fill the areas between the laces with quilting.
6 Add a second layer of wool-viscose felt to the back of the work. Stitch around the outside circle and button only, adding no further stitching between the laces.
7 Wash in hot water to shrink the wool-viscose felt.
8 The water-soluble thread dissolves and only the cotton thread stitching remains. Because the wool-viscose felt shrinks the pieces of Scoubidou lace are pushed into an arch around the button at the center.

Pucker Up (far left) uses a variation of the "doughnuts" technique (see the right side section of the diagram on page 18). Pieces of Scoubidou (lanyard)lacing were stitched to the underside of the circles with water-soluble thread, but tails of the laces were left sticking out at the outside edge. See also **Odd One Out** on page 18.

The same technique was adapted to make *Twister* (left). Here, Scoubidou laces were replaced with cotton cord, which was couched to the underside of the fabric, radiating from the button. A twin needle was used with cotton thread (see cording in the Glossary, page 126). The fabric was then layered on to wool-viscose felt and the circles stitched only around the circumference – the whole area within the circle (including around the button at the center) was left unstitched, free from the felt. The background areas around the circles were quilted and the piece was then washed to encourage shrinkage.

The shrunken wool-viscose felt behind the circle shapes caused the top fabric to become crumpled mounds. Before drying, I twisted or turned the button, encouraging the fabric to lie in a spiraling swirl. When dry, the button was secured to the back, leaving the fabric swirling around the center.

Squaring Up (see page 7) and *Moonshadow* (below) are examples in which the same technique was used but in sections of a traditional patchwork block. Scoubidou laces were also used to add dimension in **Ammonoidia** (see page 43) and **Wound Up** (see page 44).

From left to right:
Pucker Up (C. June Barnes)
23½" x 50" (60 x 127cm)

Twister (C. June Barnes)
12" x 22" (30 x 56cm)

Moonshadow (C. June Barnes)
8" x 12" (20 x 30cm)

These pieces were created by exploring variations on the doughnuts shrinkage technique.

Surface Embellishment

Dimension can be achieved by adding extra bits or items to the work which sit proud of the surface. These could take the shape of leaves (see Leslie Morgan's *Fall*, below), pinwheels or, as in the case of Leslie's *Chaos* (opposite), letters.

The additions are made independently using a heavy interfacing such as Pelmet Vilene in the layers to give rigidity, and attached to the surface of the piece. This can be done in a variety of ways:

- It can be stitched or stuck directly on to the surface – this option giving the least amount of dimension.
- It can be attached to the surface using a spacer such as a bead or piece of acrylic rod or tubing.
- It can be attached to a strip of stiff plastic which creates a spring-like hinge not unlike those used for sticking stamps into an album. This has the advantage of adding movement to the attachment.

Right:
Chaos (Leslie Morgan, 1995)
24" x 24" (60 x 60cm)
Letters, backed with stiffener, are applied to the surface of the quilt, layer on layer.

Opposite:
Fall, detail (Leslie Morgan, 1996)
Dimension is achieved by stitching leaves to the surface. Further dimension can be added by using spacers or hinges instead of stich.

Manipulating the Plane

Weaving Strips

Traditional basket-making and weaving techniques using strips of fabric have been widely employed in textiles for both flat and three-dimensional items. Jodie Hatcher is a metalworker who uses metal strips to make the most inspirational shapes. Ingrid Press makes beautiful contemporary baskets. My *Woven Tub* (above) was inspired by their work.

Coiling

Coiling is another basketry process that lends itself to textiles. In *Coiled Up* (left) continuous strips of fabric cut on the bias were wrapped and stitched around piping cord and then coiled around an inner tube to create a cylindrical container.

Above:
Woven Tub (C. June Barnes)
20" x 4" x 12" (50 x 10 x 30cm)

Left:
Coiled Up (C. June Barnes)
10" x 3" (26 x 8cm)

Right:
What's Yellow and Black...?
(C. June Barnes)
3" x 3" x 3½" (8x 8 x 9cm)

Folding

Scoubidou braids

These constructions are based on the Scoubidou (lanyard) craft of knotting and plaiting, which was the rage when I was a child, and which is still a very popular hobby today. The techniques are very similar to those used in macramé and corn dollies. They lend themselves to exploration with strips of stitched textiles of varying widths and thickness. Try out these techniques with card or firm paper before working on a project.

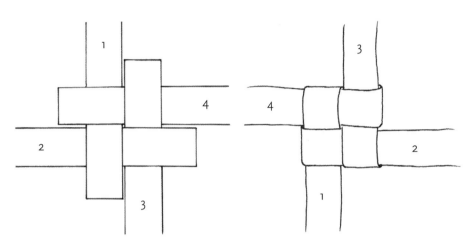

Basic technique
Number four strips 1 to 4 and place them in the starting position as shown in the diagrams above. In *What's Yellow and Black...?* (below) the color of the strips alternated between yellow and black.

Round 1. Working counterclockwise, start with strip 1 and fold the strips back on themselves. Leave the first strip lying loosely because the fourth strip needs to be slipped underneath it. Work in numerical sequence 1, 2, 3, 4. Pull all strips firm and square once the sequence is complete.

Round 2. Next, work clockwise, starting with strip 4. Fold the strips back on themselves as before, but this time reverse the sequence: 4, 3, 2, 1, leaving the first strip (4), lying loosely so that the fourth strip (1) can be slipped underneath it. Pull all strips firm and square at the end of the sequence.

Repeat these two rounds until you run out of strip. Secure.

Scoubidou 1
What's Yellow and Black...?

Two pairs of double-sided strips 1½" (3.8cm) wide and about 5' (1.5m) long were made.

These had Fast2Fuse interfacing in the layers. Contrasting fabrics work best; patterns on fabrics are lost, although stripes along the length of the strip and dots would have an impact.

The strips were the same color on both sides, but experiment with other color combinations. In this case, the thickness of the strips and the length used produced a stack only 4" (10cm) high.

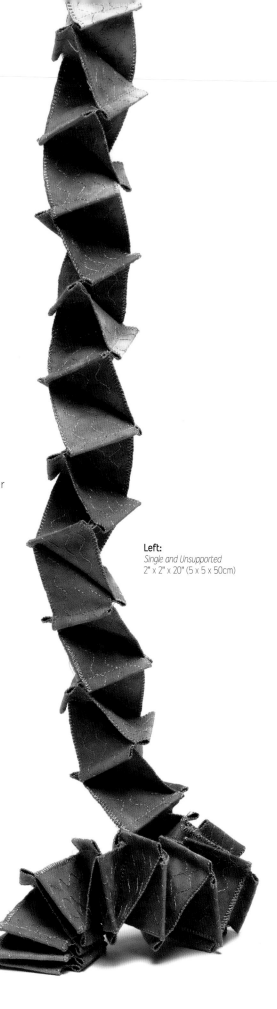

Scoubidou 2 *Single and Unsupported*

In the piece shown right, two pairs of fabric strips were bonded to one another, over-sewn at the edges and decoratively stitched along the lengths. They were then folded as a single pair with the folds stitched to add stability. A single pair of strips can only be woven in one direction, clockwise or anticlockwise, which results in a twist to the finished strip.

Scoubidou 3 *Split Down the Middle*

Using longer lengths and layers with no stiffening produces a longer, woven rope. In this pair, shown left, one has a support rod in the center (an old knitting needle), while the other is unsupported and flexible.

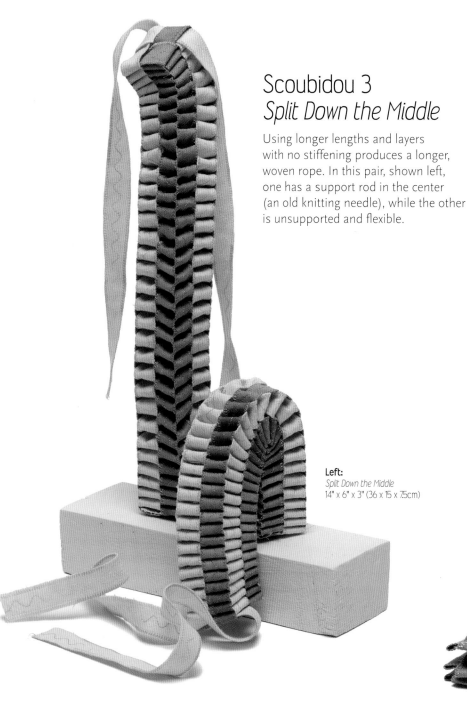

Left:
Split Down the Middle
14" x 6" x 3" (36 x 15 x 7.5cm)

Left:
Single and Unsupported
2" x 2" x 20" (5 x 5 x 50cm)

Scoubidou 4 *Together*

This is essentially a double of *What's Yellow and Black...?* (see page 25), based on the Scoubidou brick stitch. Prepare six strips, two of which need to be twice the length of the other four. Number the two long strips 1 and 2 and the four others 3, 4, 5 and 6. Arrange them as illustrated in the diagram below.

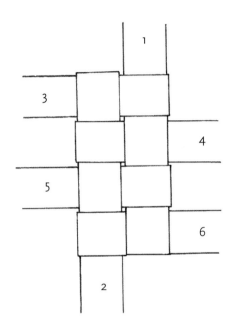

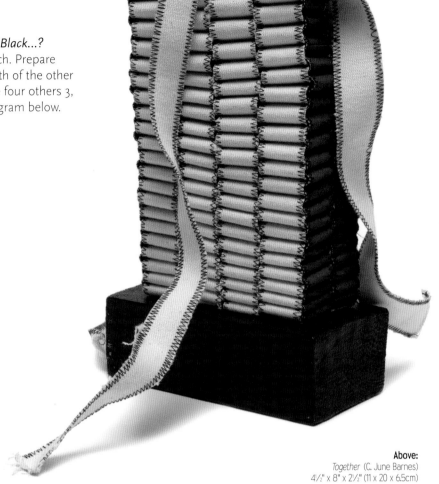

Above:
Together (C. June Barnes)
4½" x 8" x 2½" (11 x 20 x 6.5cm)

1 Using the alignment in the diagram, bring strip 1 down the length of the group, and take strip 2 up to the top. Lay these two strips loosely.
2 Take 3 and lay it from left to right over 2 and under 1. Take 4 and lay it from right to left over 1 and under 2. Take 5 and lay it from left to right over 2 and under 1. Take 6 and lay it from right to left over 1 and under 2. Lastly, tighten 1 and 2, ending up with the layout shown in the diagram right.
3 Repeat the process, but now first take strip 1 up and bring strip 2 down.
4 Then weave 3 from right to left over 1 and under 2. 4 from left to right over 2 and under 1. 5 from right to left over 1 and under 2. 6 from left to right over 2 and under 1.
5 Firm up 1 and 2 and repeat these steps until you run out of strip.

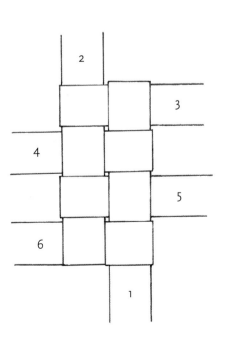

Fortunity

This modular structure (left) was made using the children's paper fortune-teller origami-based game as a starting point. This form of origami is also known as chatterbox, cootie catcher, and salt cellar, and an Internet search will reveal amazing creative possibilities. Three different fabrics were used; two layers of each were fused to one another, and five different sizes of the module were made. These were fixed to a canvas using a glue gun.

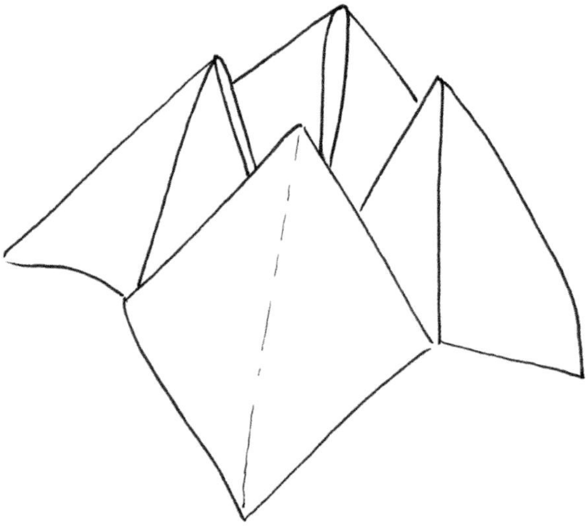

Left:
Fortunity (C. June Barnes)
6½" x 30¼" (16 x 77cm)
Embossing powders add an
additional texture, which is only
apparent on close inspection.

Below:
Fortunitree (C. June Barnes)
10" x 10" x 12" (25 x 25 x 30cm)

Fortunitree

This structure was made of the same fortune-teller units, the size diminishing upwards. A range of fabrics, dyed using an exchange between rust and green, were used.

Gathering

Large pieces of quilted or stitched layers can be manipulated by gathering, pleating, smocking and so on to create added depth.

My inspirations for *Hotting Up* (right) were the furrows of ploughed fields and the ripples left on a sandy beach after the tide has gone out.

A long, flat piece of stitched layers, over 16' (5m) long, was dyed using a gradation of red to yellow with Procion dye. Lengths of piping cord, which had also been dyed to blend, were used to gather up the stitched panel using big stitches, drawing the work up to about a third of its original length. The result can be changed for variety from time to time by rearranging the gathers – rather like the ripples left in the sand on the beach after the tide has gone out.

The method is very versatile. Other materials, such as metal rods, wire and wooden dowels, could be used to support the gathers. Varying the width of the work or the rigidity of the gathered surface pieces will result in very different appearances. For instance, *Loopholes* (left) is a very long, narrow piece of quilted layers which has been looped and stitched into a formation similar to gathering – but no gathering thread was used. This is a free-form installation that can be arranged in whichever way suits.

Left and below:
Loopholes, and detail
(C. June Barnes)
120" x 8" x 4" (3m x 20 x 10cm)
This piece uses a similar gathering technique as *Hotting Up* (opposite) but no gathering thread was used.

Left:
Hotting Up (C June Barnes)
30" x 66" (75 x 178cm)
Gathered and stitched silk and
cotton batting.

Below:
Inspiration for *Hotting Up* — ripples
on a beach and ploughed furrows
in a field.

Smocking

Traditionally, the embroidery technique of smocking involves the use of a single layer of lightweight fabric which is gathered together into regular pleats with a thread, and the pleated fabric is then stitched in place using a variety of patterns. For *Tagged* (below and opposite) these traditional smocking techniques were adapted to manipulate a large piece of quilted layers. Cable ties were used for the stitching, and these were spray painted so that they suited the piece. The piece is double sided – both sides having an interesting surface.

Left and right:
Tagged (C. June Barnes)
41" x 56" (105 x 142cm)
Smocking, using cable ties to produce strong, large "stitches" as shown in this detail of the back (left) and detail of the front (right).

Arranging the Plane

Right:
Aspirations (C. June Barnes)
48" (120cm) high with
8—14" (20—35cm) circles
With stacking, a relatively simple
shape can be repeated and
becomes three-dimensional.

Stacking and Layering

Aspirations (opposite), *Cascade 1: Squares* (see page 36) and *Cascade 2: Circles* (see page 61) are examples of quilted layers being layered or stacked in various ways. Individual units can also be stacked to create a structure. See *Ascension* on page 57 and *Upper Reaches* on page 103.

Aspirations

A number of discs in graded sizes were stitched using layers of fabric, wool-viscose felt, and Pelmet Vilene. These were dyed and shrunk to achieve an irregular surface. Holes were made in the centers using large eyelets, and these were threaded on to pieces of acrylic rod for support. Rubber washers were used to space the discs as required. In the image shown, these were arranged on three separate rods, but with closer spacing all the discs could be put on to a single rod for a very different look.

Cascade 1: Squares

This piece is made of ten layers, nine of which have a window through which the previous layers can be seen. Each window, working forwards from the back layer, increases in size, revealing just a strip of the area surrounding the window of the previous layer. The windows are cut only on three sides, the fourth side forming a hinge, which allows it to flap or drop forward, echoing the decreasing windows in a cascade. Layers of ¼" (6mm) foam were placed in between the layers to add depth. The fabrics used were dyed using the exchange or cross-over method of dyeing, which is explained in my book *Stitching to Dye in Quilt Art* (see Recommended Reading, page 127).

Materials:
- Backing board, artist's canvas, or framework to support the whole structure.
- Ten pieces of cotton batting (stabilized is best but not too thick as it needs to drape), 24" (60cm) square (includes 2" (5cm) seam or adjustment margin).
- ¼" (6mm) firm foam sheet to use as spacers between the layers and suitable adhesive. Foam board would also work but is more fragile.
  Note: Measurements of the pieces will change after stitching and quilting, which means that the size of the foam will need to be adjusted accordingly.
- Ten fabric pieces. The amount required is not the same for all layers. The full square need not be sandwiched or quilted – just the essential central areas. This area gets larger as you work through the layers, so progressively more fabric is needed for later squares where two pieces 24" (60cm) square are needed. Fabric for the binding needs to be taken into account.
- Fusible web – normal weight (not essential – layers can be tacked or basted instead).

Method:
1. Place an 3" (8cm) square of the first fabric at the center of a piece of batting and quilt the area within the square. Note that the full 24" (60cm) squares need not be covered with fabric or quilted as most of the area will be hidden under subsequent layers.
2. Cut two 5" (13cm) squares from the second fabric and bond or tack these to both sides at the center of the second batting piece.

3. Mark a 2" (5cm) square at the center of the 13cm (5in) square, leaving a 1½"(4cm) border of fabric around the marked area. Cut along only three sides of the 2" (5cm) square, creating a window with the fourth edge attached to form a hinge. Stay stitching inside the cutting line (just under the width of the satin stitch to be used), before cutting the window makes over-sewing the edges easier.
4. Using a suitable thread, over-sew all cut edges of the hinged window and frame using zigzag, satin stitch, or similar. Use the same thread on the top and in the bobbin.
5. Quilt the flap from the underside/back of the layer. When this window section flaps forwards, the back will be visible at the front. Quilt an area of at least 1" (2.5cm) wide around the frame of the window from the front. You may prefer to do the quilting before cutting and over-sewing the edges. If you do, remember which side of the work will be visible and quilt from that side.
6. Repeat steps 2 to 5, increasing the hinged center by 2" (5cm) on each new batting square. The two squares of fabric at the center of the batting are always 3" (8cm) larger than the flapping window.
7. When all layers have been worked, and starting with the block with the largest window, press from the wrong side and trim all pieces to the same size. Stitch the binding to the outside edges with the same fabric used on the block – at least ¼" (6mm) in at the front edge using 2" (5cm) strips (straight or bias as preferred). Glue strips of foam around the outside edges, about 2" (5cm) narrower than the border area around the window so that the foam is not visible when viewing from the front.
8. Work through all blocks, matching and trimming the measurements to the last block. As the area backed with foam becomes larger, it may be easier to use a square of foam rather than strips, cutting the window area away.
9. Wrap the binding around all layers – fabric/batting and foam – and secure with stitch or adhesive as you prefer.
10. Glue the first, windowless piece to the backing board using a glue gun. Then add the other pieces to the stack, gluing each layer in place, starting with the smallest window and ending with the largest.

When presented vertically, the windows flap forwards and downwards. Beads or similar ornaments could be attached to assist gravity.

Left:
Cascade 1: Squares (C. June Barnes)
20" x 20" (51 x 51cm)
Tongues of quilted fabric, dyed using the exchange method, create an optical as well as physical third dimension as the viewer is drawn into the mouth of the cascade.

Curling or Wrapping

One of the easiest ways to create a piece of three-dimensional artwork is to wrap a long piece of layered and stitched/quilted work around a supporting structure. Continuous surfaces can be arranged in a series of loops, crossings and compressions around a central support. The possibilities are endless and will be affected by the materials used – whether rigid or soft.

In its simplest form, the work is a sleeve that fits around a circular column such as Audrey Critchley's *Grave Posts* (see page 107), Inger Milburn's *Zip Tree* (see page 111) and my own *Topping Up* (see page 95). Structures such as Inger's *Looking Through* (opposite and below) may look very complex but in fact are fairly straightforward, where the folds and curls are supported on a central column. *Magic Circles* (see page 40) are further examples where circles and spirals were wrapped around a central support.

Inger Milburn's *Looking Through* is made of one long tapered piece with a couple of eye-shaped holes strategically placed. At the narrow end she made a circular hole through which she could feed a stick to hold it in place. Along the opposite edge, which was the width of the central column it was supported on, and on the long edges, she attached a few carefully placed fabric loops so that the whole could be wrapped around the central column of the stand and be secured quite firmly with the stick, then the rest was looped round in various ways, finally being secured at the end by pushing the stick through the hole. The order in which the stick goes through the loops and hole can be altered to create different effects.

Loopholes (page 30) and *Single and Unsupported* (page 26) are examples of curling. Long pieces are allowed to drape and curl into a pool formation in a fluid and flexible way.

Left and opposite:
Looking Through (Inger Milburn)
25½" x 14" (65 x 35cm)
Continuous surfaces can be
curled or wrapped around a
central support to give a
three-dimensional effect.

Spirals

There are a number of ways to draw a spiral. You can play around with strings and drawing pins, but for accuracy a little mathematics has to be involved! The Fibonacci, Archimedean and logarithmic or equiangular spirals are the most useful options.

Spirals may look complex to construct, but looking beyond what seem to be complicated calculations will reveal that they are not that difficult to draw, and are in fact fun! Because textile projects tend to be larger than a letter-size piece of paper, the scale of spirals available from a pattern or on the Internet is not big enough. You need to work with large sheets of paper (I find flip charts invaluable) and a long ruler.

Left:
Magic Circles (C. June Barnes)
39" x 12—20" (100 x 39—50cm)
Two circular pieces comprising backing, stiffener and top were layered. The lime green piece was based on an Archimedean spiral, the purple on an equiangular spiral, and the pink on concentric circles.

Fibonacci spiral

The Fibonacci sequence is named after the eponymous 12th-century Italian mathematician. There are many examples of the sequence in nature – pine cones, sunflower seed heads, and a snail's shell, to name a few. The first two Fibonacci numbers are 0 and 1, and each subsequent number is the sum of the previous two – 0, 1, 1, 2, 3, 5, 8, 13, 21 and so on.

To draw a Fibonacci spiral (shown in diagram, right):

1 Draw two small, equal squares adjacent to one another.
2 Add a square to the right of these squares, which has its measurement equal to the sum of the first two squares.
3 Continue to add a sequence of growing squares counter-clockwise.
4 Starting at the point x draw quarter circles inside the first two squares.
5 Move on to the third square and, using the inside corner of the square at y as the center draw a quarter circle, which links with the second.

Continue this pattern with all the squares to draw the Fibonacci spiral.

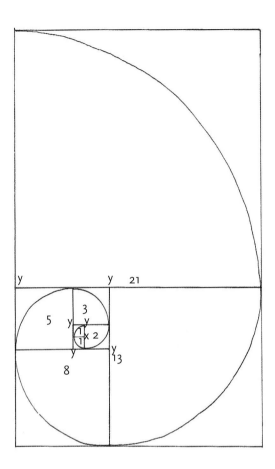

Golden Triangle spiral

An equiangular spiral (see page 42) can be drawn using the Golden Triangle in the same way as the Fibonacci sequence. The Golden Triangle is an isosceles triangle with a vertex angle of 36° and base angles of 72°. The legs are in golden ratio (proportion) to the base. If you bisect one of the base angles of 72° of such an isosceles triangle, the bisecting line divides the opposite side in a golden ratio and forms two smaller isosceles triangles.

By repeatedly bisecting the base angles of the triangles formed, new points are created that, in turn, make other Golden Triangles. The bisection process can be continued infinitely, creating an infinite number of Golden Triangles. A logarithmic or equiangular spiral can be drawn through the vertices (the blue line in the diagram, left).

The problem with Fibonacci and Golden Triangle spirals is that they are very large scale. *Ammonoidia* (see page 43), *Wound Up,* (see page 44) and *Magic Circles* (opposite) needed spirals of a smaller scale, and so I looked for alternatives.

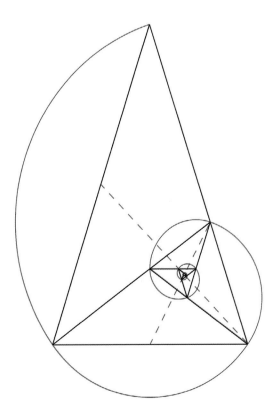

Equiangular spiral

The equiangular spiral, also known as a logarithmic spiral or growth spiral, was first discovered by René Descartes, the French mathematician, in the 17th century. Successive turnings of the spiral form a geometric progression (increasing in width) once the initial spiral is set in motion.

To draw an equiangular spiral, refer to the diagrams shown right and below right. Instructions for this process are shown in millimeters only.

1 Follow the steps as for the Archimedean spiral on page 44 until you have marked the 12th line (36mm) – the original 0.
2 Working in a counterclockwise direction, mark a point on the next 30° line (the 1st) that is 1mm more than the initial increment used (3 + 1 = 4mm). On the next line increase the previous increment by 2mm (4 + 2 = 6mm). Continue to add 1mm to the previous increment all the way around, starting with the 12th line = 36;
   + 4 = **40**; + 5 = **45**; + 6 = **51**; + 7 = **58**; + 8 = **66**; + 9 = **75**; + 10 = **85**, and so on. This is shown as a solid line in the diagram above.
3 The rate at which the spiral widens can be faster by increasing the increment at each point. For example, if the increment at each step is 2 the spiral will get wider more quickly (36; + 5 = **41**; + 7 = **48**; + 9 = **57**; + 10 = **67**; + 12 = **77**; + 14 = **91**, and so on. This is shown as a dotted line in the diagram right.
4 Join the points with a smooth curve.
5 Remove the construction lines.

Opposite:
Ammonoidia, detail (C. June Barnes)
14" x 14" (35 x 35cm)
Made using an equiangular spiral.

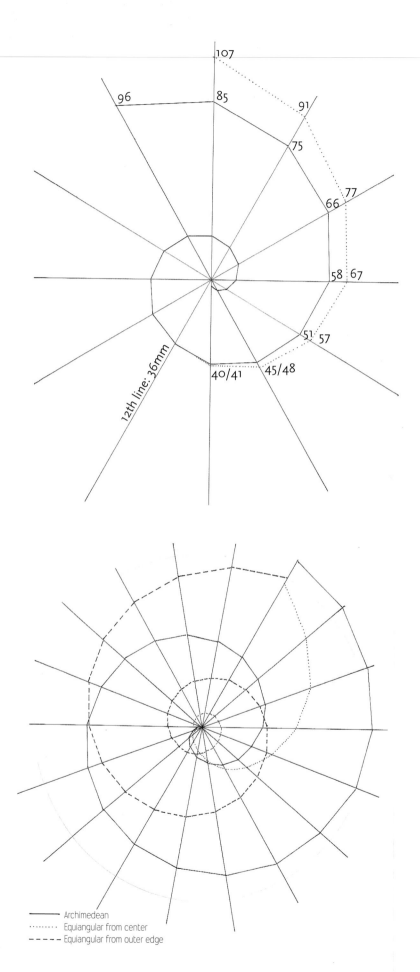

—————— Archimedean
················ Equiangular from center
– – – – – Equiangular from outer edge

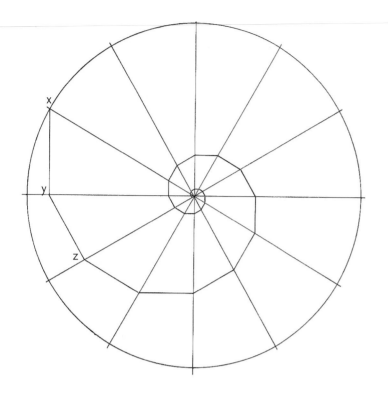

Alternative equiangular spiral

Another way to draw an equiangular spiral starts from the outside and works its way inwards. This is useful when you know the size of the outside circle.

To draw the spiral, refer to the diagram above.

1 Draw a circle of the radius you require.
2 Divide the circle into a grid of 12 radiating lines 30° apart as before.
3 Select a point on the outside of the circle where it meets one of the radiating lines (x) and, working in an anticlockwise direction, draw a perpendicular line (at right angles) from the next radius at y back to x. Use a set square to do this.
4 From a point on the third radiating line (z), draw a perpendicular line to meet the first perpendicular line drawn at y.
5 Continue this process as long as you can, until you reach the central point.
6 Round all the lines into a smooth curve and erase the construction lines.

See the diagram opposite for the same sequence with a grid of radiating lines 20° apart (indicated with a dashed line).

Right:
Wound Up (C. June Barnes) 19½" x
19½" (50 x 50cm)
This design is based on an
Archimedian spiral.

Archimedean spiral

The Archimedean spiral is named after Archimedes, the Greek mathematician from the 3rd century BC. It is also known as the arithmetic spiral and is distinguished from the equiangular or logarithmic spiral (see page 42) by the fact that successive turnings of the spiral have a constant separation distance, while in a logarithmic spiral these distances form a geometric progression. For the purpose of this exercise, I have used an increment of ⅛" (3mm), but any number can be used. To draw an Archimedean spiral, refer to the diagrams shown right and below right. Instructions are shown in millimeters only.

1 Draw a grid based on an array of 12 radiating lines (30° divisions of a circle).
2 The center is 0.
3 Start on one line and mark a point ⅛" (3mm) from the center.
4 Moving in an anticlockwise direction, move to the next 30° line and mark a point 6mm from the center.
5 Continue working anticlockwise in this way, marking a point on each successive line, where the distance from the central point is increased by 3mm from the line before (3, 6, 9, 12, 15, 18, 21 and so on).
6 Join the points and convert into a smooth curve.
7 Remove the construction grid.

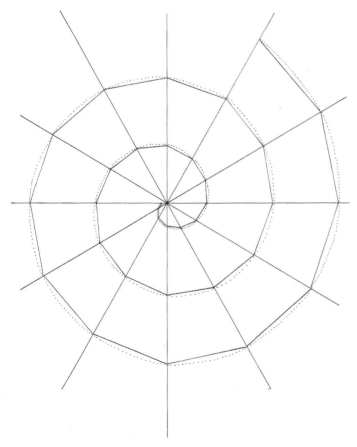

Magic Circles

Layer two circular pieces (backing, interfacing, and top). Mark an Archimedean spiral on one and an equiangular spiral on the other. To do this, to draw the spirals on layout paper, pin to the layers and stitch through. Tear the paper away, leaving the spirals marked on both sides of the layered materials.

Stitch about 4mm from the first line of stitching and cut the spiral out between the stitched lines. Oversew the outside edges with satin stitch and add a bias strip sleeve to the inside edge to accommodate a supporting metal rod.

Cut a small circle from the center of a third layered circular piece. Divide the rest into two concentric circles forming two rings of equal width. Stitch about 3mm along each side of the marked line before cutting first along the radius and then between the rows of stitching, forming two split rings. Join these circles at one of the straight cut edges making one continuous strip. Finish in the same way as the spirals and attach to a supporting rod.

Right:
Fantasy Trees (Marion Glover)
22—7" x 8½—6½"
(57—18 x 21—16cm)
Constructed using a combination of Archimedean and equiangular spirals.

Stretching and Extending

Sometimes all that is needed to create and support a shape is gravity. The work needs to be reasonably substantial for this to work on its own, but lighter pieces could be weighted to assist.

Stretching — *Inner Spin*

A number of circles were cut out of Pelmet Vilene and a small circle was cut out at the center of each. The circles were then cut along the radii. A backing of cotton fabric was fused on to one side and a layer of cotton batting was added to the other side. This top surface was covered with a variety of solid-colored fabric using foundation piecing.

When all the discs were finished they were joined to one another at the cut edges, attaching edge A–B on one disc to edge C–D on the next, forming a continuous spiraling corkscrew (see diagram on page 59).

Right:
Inner Spin, detail (C. June Barnes)
85" x 14" (200 x 35cm)
These two-dimensional circles are rendered three-dimensional using gravity to stretch them into shape.

Extending —
Stretching a Point

A long piece, approximately 6½' (2m) long, 17" (43cm) wide at the bottom and tapering to 9" (23cm) at the top, was cut from a sandwich of a top fabric fused to cotton batting on the front of Pelmet Vilene with a backing fabric fused to the other side. Slits were cut through all layers at regular intervals at the sides and center (see x and y in the figure below). The layers were quilted and all edges over-sewn with satin stitch.

To get the maximum effect, a piece of pipe was inserted in a sleeve at the wide end/bottom. When suspended the weight of the pipe causes the work to expand at the slits, which can be arranged to suit.

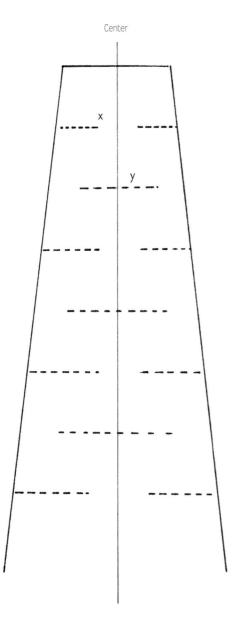

Center

x

y

Right:
Stretching a Point, detail
C. June Barnes)
100" x 16—6" (250 x 40—15cm)
Two-dimensional forms can
be extended to create a
three-dimensional shape.

Twisting

Above:
Möbius Stitched (C. June Barnes)
18" x 9½" (45 x 24cm)
Heavy interfacing has been used between the quilting to maintain the shape.

A Möbius strip is a surface with only one side and only one boundary component. It was discovered independently by the German mathematicians August Ferdinand Möbius and Johann Benedict Listing in 1858.

The Möbius strip has some interesting properties. If you draw a line from the join down the middle it will meet back at the join, but on the apparent other side. If you continued the line it will meet the starting point and will be double the length of the original strip. Equally, if you were to follow the edge of the strip with a colored pen you will end at the same point where you began because there is only one boundary.

How to make a Möbius loop

Using the illustration shown right for guidance, take a strip of paper (A–B–b–a) and give it a half-twist. With the twist in place, join the ends of the strip together so that A meets b and B meets a, forming a loop. The twist can be either left-handed or right-handed. Note that in this example the loop has one shaded side purely to illustrate the process. If both sides of the strip are not the same there will be no continuity (see *Striped Möbius Loop* below).

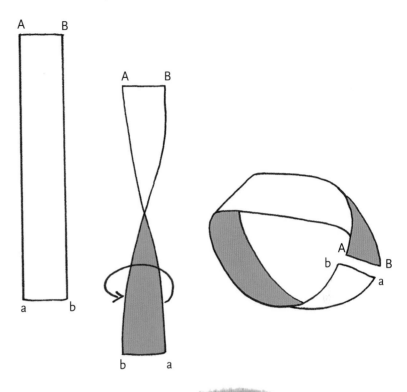

Right:
Striped Möbius Loop
(C. June Barnes)
10" x 9" x 5½" (25 x 23 x 14cm)
In order to get the fabrics to match at the join, the floral fabric is on top of the striped one although the white strip is in the middle of both sides.

There is enormous potential for creating structures based on the Möbius loop. Try experimenting with paper strips to discover the possibilities:

- A loop with an odd-number of half-twists will have only one surface and one boundary.
- Instead of the half-twist, try a full twist. A loop twisted an even number of half-twists will have two surfaces and two boundaries, and is not a Möbius loop. Only an odd-number of half-twists will result in only one surface and one boundary.
- Try changing the shape of the strip so that it is irregular in width.
- Once you have made a strip, cut it in half along its length to see what happens. If you cut a strip with an odd number of half-twists in half along its length, you will have a longer strip, with the same number of loops as there are half-twists in the original. If a strip with an even number of half-twists is cut in half along its length, the result is two conjoined strips, each with the same number of twists as the original.

- A strip with three half-twists when cut into two lengthwise results in a trefoil knot.

There are a few things to bear in mind when using textiles to make a Möbius loop. For example, the color, piecing and stitching or quilting all need to be the same. The **Striped Möbius Loop** (see page 49) illustrates the necessary construction. When you look at the pieced strips side by side they are identical. However, when you lay them wrong sides together you will find that the central white strip is identical on both sides, but that the striped fabric is backed by the floral fabric, and the floral fabric has the striped fabric behind it. This allows for a continuation of the same fabric when the loop is joined. It is also necessary to include some stiffening in the layers to maintain the shape. **Möbius Stitched** (see page 48) has a heavy Vilene in between the independently quilted sides.

The following variation presents further opportunities.

Below:
Chastity Begins at Home
(C. June Barnes)
14" x 10" x 10" (35 x 25 x 25cm)
Starting with the cross shape shown in the diagrams opposite, a T-shaped Möbius loop is created.

The Möbius loop using a "T" in its simplest formation – joining B to B and then looping the long strip through the ring formed and joining A to the B link. This offers an intriguing structure, which surprisingly has only a single plane and a single boundary. This will become clear when the edge of the assembled structure is over-sewn; it can be stitched in one, continuous action. In the example below, stitched Fast2Fuse was used as the inner layer and milliners' brim wire was stitched to the edge. Try introducing a half-twist to one or other of the loops before making the joins, or indeed both, and see what happens.

Möbius Slit (above) is a wide strip that has been slit into narrow strips in the center area without cutting to the end. The two intact ends were given a half-twist and joined to one another. It would be interesting to cut the narrow strips through, leaving only one end still attached, then giving them each a half-twist before joining them to another band at the end, then making another twist before joining the broad ends.

Three-dimensional Geometric Shapes

Receptacle-like shapes can be formed by manipulating a single plane. It is worth first working through the following examples using paper to see how they work. While these at first seem to be quite utilitarian, they can be used as modules for more artistic creations. See Sandra Grusd's *Colourdance* (below) and my own *Pure Fantasy: Dodecahedron* (see page 73) which has an outer layer of pentagon-based receptacles.

Below:
Colourdance (Sandra Grusd)
A combination of two constructed shapes, one with a square base (see page 54) and the other with a triangular base (see page 87).

Squares

Containers

1 Make a piece about 12" (30cm) square using Pelmet Vilene in the layers for rigidity. Do not make the sandwich too thick – it needs to fold gently but firmly. Finish the edges in whichever way suits.

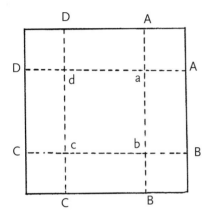

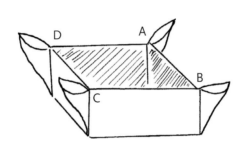

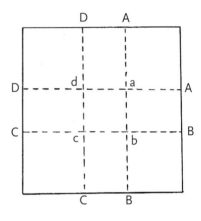

2 Mark points A, B, C and D equidistant from the corners as shown above.

3 Fold the points at the corners – A to A, B to B, C to C and D to D, and sew or join in some other way along the line A–a, B–b, C–c and D–d (above).

4 Adjusting the distance between the points at the corners changes the dimensions of the container: increasing the distance from the corners results in a deeper container (above); decreasing it makes it shallower.

Above:
In the box above left the corners have been turned inwards. The box above right shows the corner pouches sticking outwards with the points folded down.

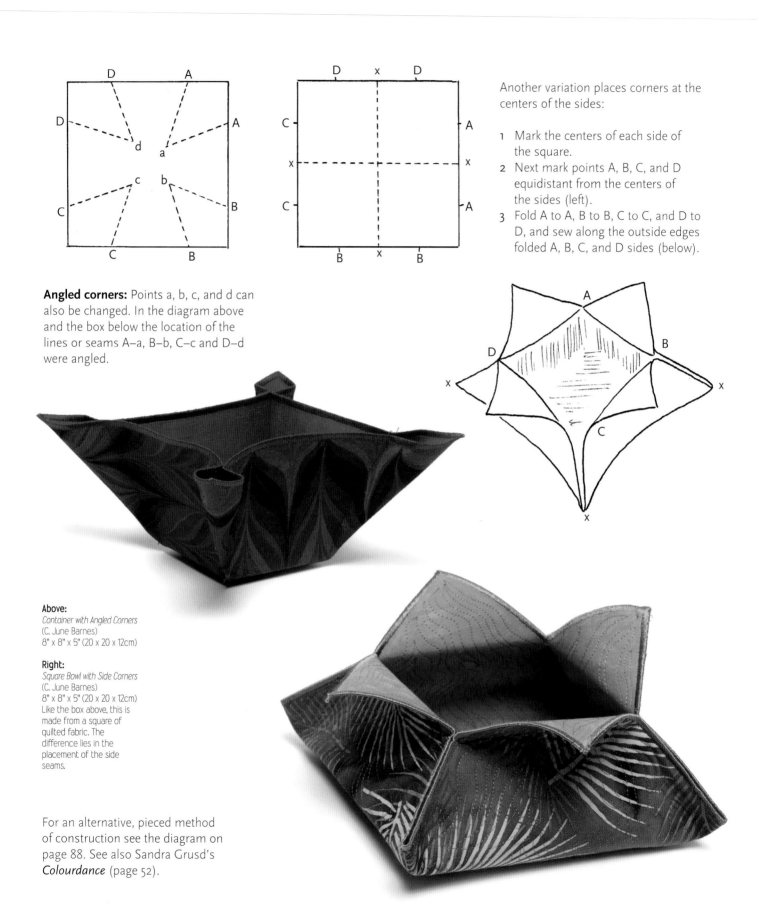

Another variation places corners at the centers of the sides:

1 Mark the centers of each side of the square.
2 Next mark points A, B, C, and D equidistant from the centers of the sides (left).
3 Fold A to A, B to B, C to C, and D to D, and sew along the outside edges folded A, B, C, and D sides (below).

Angled corners: Points a, b, c, and d can also be changed. In the diagram above and the box below the location of the lines or seams A–a, B–b, C–c and D–d were angled.

Above:
Container with Angled Corners
(C. June Barnes)
8" x 8" x 5" (20 x 20 x 12cm)

Right:
Square Bowl with Side Corners
(C. June Barnes)
8" x 8" x 5" (20 x 20 x 12cm)
Like the box above, this is made from a square of quilted fabric. The difference lies in the placement of the side seams.

For an alternative, pieced method of construction see the diagram on page 88. See also Sandra Grusd's *Colourdance* (page 52).

Pillow form

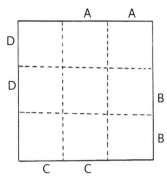

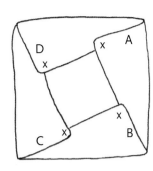

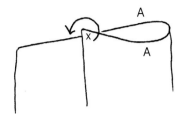

1 Divide the sides of a square into thirds and mark the edges. Now fold the sides on themselves, folding A to A, B to B, C to C, and D to D.

2 When making the fold, take the corner over to the other side of the edge so that the connection lies flat, not upright.

3 Stitch in place at that point, x, in diagram. When all sides are folded and secured you end up with a pillow form (shown below).

Variations: Try making the join upright instead of flat, and change the size of the initial fold.

Right:
Pillow Form (C. June Barnes)
8" x 8" x 4" (20 x 20 x 10cm)

Cross

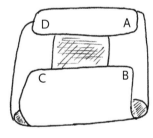

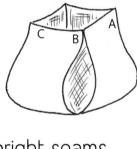

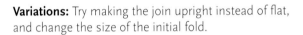

Flat seams

Cut out the corners of a square that has been divided into thirds and mark the ends of the "arms" as shown left. Arch the arms so that A lies flat onto A, B on B, C on C, and D on D (above).

Upright seams

Folding the arms in the same way but connecting them with an upright or pointed corner creates a more box-like structure (see above).

Variations: Change the proportions. For example, longer arms to the cross will make taller containers, or add extensions to the ends of the arms, such as triangles or circles, which could be folded back or twisted.

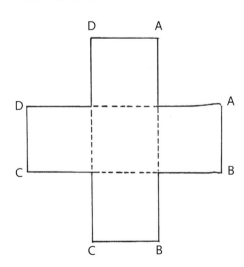

Pinwheels

Pinwheels can be attached to the surface of a piece to achieve dimension or multiples can be combined to form a molecular structure. In *Ascension* (opposite) larger-scale pinwheels of decreasing dimensions were stacked into an ascending tower.

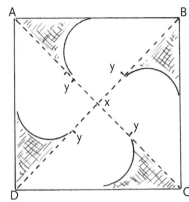

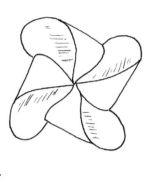

From a square

Following the diagrams above left, take up a square piece that has been slit inwards at the corners as far as y (approximately two-thirds from the edge). Finish all cut edges with satin stitch. Fold the corners marked * over to the center (x) and secure. In the diagrams above right the points of the sails are rounded.

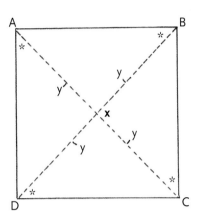

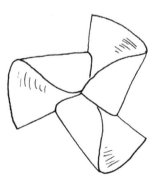

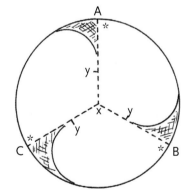

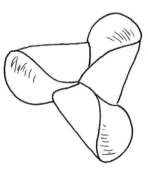

From a circle

Both of the examples made from a square can also be made using a circle – the divisions, trims, and joins are exactly the same. One advantage of using a circle is that it can easily be divided into sections other than four, which means that there is no restriction on the number of sails. The lower sections of *Ascension* (opposite) have more than four sails. Fewer sections (three in the diagrams above left) or more sections can be made by dividing the circle into the required number of segments. The unmarked points of the sails can also be rounded (as shown in the diagrams above right).

Ascension is a collection of circular pinwheels decreasing in size as they ascend the column. The pinwheels are organized in pairs – one with the sail corners pointed, the other rounded and turning in the opposite direction from its pair. The uppermost pair of pinwheels has only three sails. The numbers of sails increases as the pinwheels get larger, with the lowest pair having seven. The pinwheels have eyelets at their centers and are mounted on an acrylic rod. When a current of air is directed at the structure the pinwheels move in both clockwise and counterclockwise directions.

Left:
Ascension (C. June Barnes)
18" x 8—4" (45 x 20—10cm)
Constructed from a combination of pointed and rounded pinwheels.

Circles

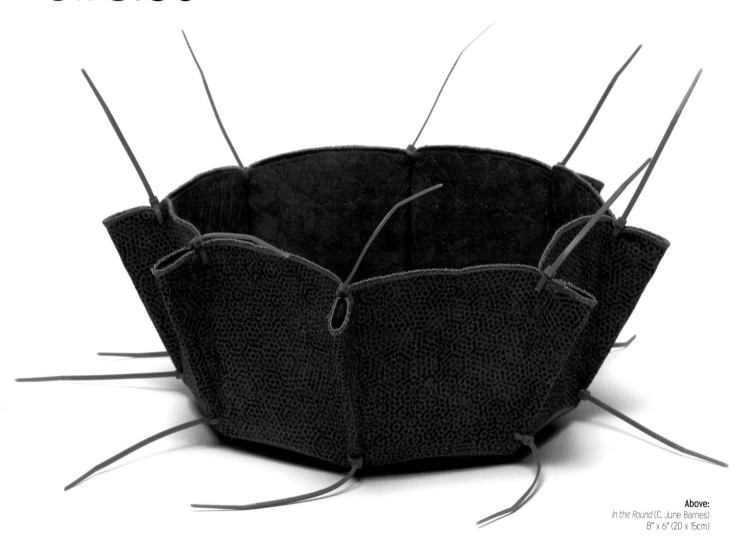

Above:
In the Round (C. June Barnes)
8" x 6" (20 x 15cm)

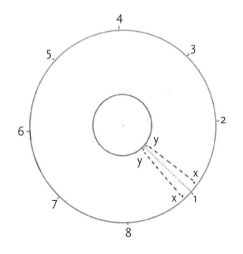

Containers

The constructions explained in Squares on pages 53–55 can be adapted using circles instead. *In the Round* (above) is a circle cut from a sandwich of top and backing fabrics bonded to Fast2Fuse. A smaller, internal circle was marked as the base of the container and a row of satin stitch used to show its perimeter (see diagram, left). After quilting, the circumference was divided into eight equal points. Cable ties were used to make a pleat 1" (2.5cm) on either side of these points (x) and used to make a small pleat – less than ½" (1.3cm) – straddling a corresponding point on the edge of the base circle (y). The pleats were pressed and the center encouraged to lie flat.

Flares

Two or more identical circles cut along the radius and joined to one another along the cut radius create interesting forms. An adaptation of this technique was used in *Inner Spin* on page 46.

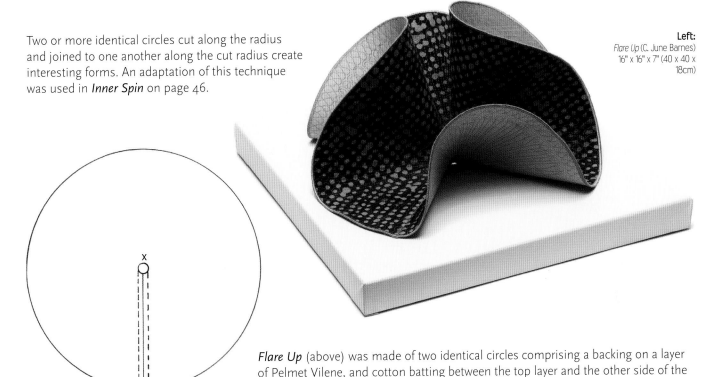

Left:
Flare Up (C. June Barnes)
16" x 16" x 7" (40 x 40 x 18cm)

Flare Up (above) was made of two identical circles comprising a backing on a layer of Pelmet Vilene, and cotton batting between the top layer and the other side of the Pelmet Vilene. The straight of the grain of the backing and top were lined up. Less rigidity and thickness of these layers would result in different effects. A small circle (x) ½" (1.3cm) was cut from the center of each circle, and a line drawn on the straight of the grain along the radius between the inner and outer circles (x–y) (see diagram, left). The seam allowance or stitching lines were marked on either side of this cutting line – extending from the edges of the small central circle. The circles were quilted before they were joined, leaving an area unquilted along the stitching line. The quilting was completed after the circles were joined to one another along the cut edges. The edges were finished with satin stitch.

Below right:
Lifted Up (C. June Barnes)
14" x 4" (35 x 10cm)

Lifted Up

Two circles of the same size were made with Pelmet Vilene included in the layers for rigidity. A circle was cut out of the center of one. An extended circle or oval-shaped aperture with the same circumference as the circle cut from the center of the first circle was cut from the middle of the second circle. The outside edges of the main circles were over-sewn and the two circles joined to one another along the perimeters of the center holes. The center shapes could be pieced following the D-Form principles (see page 99).

Stacked or layered

Multiple circles can be stacked – see *Aspirations* on page 34 – or assembled so that they fall down over one another in a tumbling drop as in *Cascade 2: Circles*.

Cascade 2: Circles is an array of double-sided extended circles (see diagram, right). The areas A, B, C, D of each part were stitched, about 1" (2.5cm) apart, to the background along the marked diameters A–B and C–D. As the fabric on the underside of the upper section flaps forward and is visible, the choice of colors, fabrics, and quilting needs to be kept in mind. It is always best to quilt from the front. Using densely stitched lines radiating from the middle of each half piece caused the circles to flare slightly. The edges were over-sewn with satin stitch. The assembled piece was mounted to a backing board, allowing the semi-circles to cascade forward when presented in the vertical position.

Other shapes could be used instead of circles, or the circles could gradually decrease in size. The orientation could be horizontal (see below), with a stiffener added to the layers to support this arrangement; the semi-circles would then stick outwards like the pages of a book.

Tip: To assemble a sandwich of matching pairs of circles (or any other shape), first mark the pattern on one of the fabrics, then pin the two fabrics, stiffener (if included) and the batting together uncut. Once pinned or basted together, stitch along the marked pattern line, quilt and cut through all layers when the quilting is done.

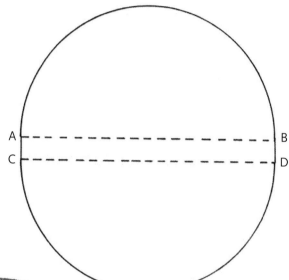

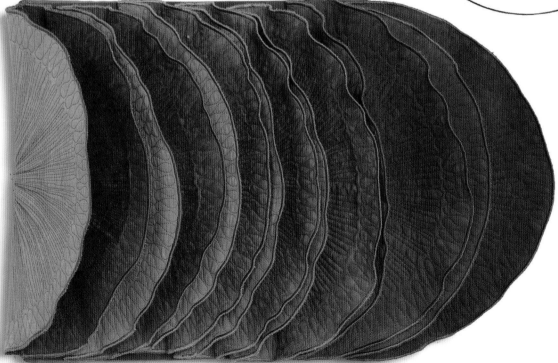

Left:
Cascade 2: Circles, horizontal view (C. June Barnes)
19" x 12" (48 x 30cm)

Right:
Cascade 2: Circles, vertical
view (C. June Barnes)
19" x 12" (48 x 30cm))

Cones

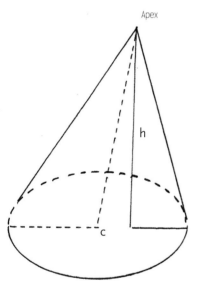

A cone is a three-dimensional geometric shape that tapers smoothly from a flat, usually (but not always) circular base to a point called the apex or vertex. The axis of a cone is the straight line (usually right angled) that would pass through the apex and the center of the circle at the base (see diagram, left).

Such a cone is called "right circular," meaning that the axis passes through the center of the base at right angles to its plane, and that the base is a circle. In an oblique cone (see diagram, below left) the axis does not pass through the center of the base at a right angle. Reducing the height (h) of the axis produces a shallower cone, which if inverted and with no base, is more bowl-like.

A section of a circle can be used to make a cone that has no base, like an empty ice-cream cone; the smaller the section, the more acute the cone.

Right:
Conical bottles from *Bottle Mania!*
(see pages 92—93) (C. June Barnes)
8—14" x 6—8" (20—35 x 15—20cm)
These pieces show both right-circular
and oblique cones.

Flower formations such as foxgloves, Weigelia, and red hot pokers were the inspiration for *Cascade 3: Cones*. A backing fabric was bonded to Pelmet Vilene. Circles of the top/outer fabric were stitched to the other side and small cones were made by cutting these circles into four quadrants. If size is essential to the finished project, make allowance in the size of the circle for seams on the cutting edge. After adding decorative stitching and finishing the edges, the straight sides of the quadrants were overlapped slightly and glued to one another. Alternatively, the edges could be handstitched. The cones were attached to a layer of jute using strong thread so that they tumbled over one another. This was fixed to an artist's stretched canvas over a curved framework of chicken wire so that it bowed to the front.

Left:
Shallow Cone Bowl (C. June
Barnes)
12" x 3" (30 x 8cm)

Shallow cone

A circle can be transformed into a bowl-like (or hat-like) disc by adding darts or removing sectors, as for **Shallow Cone Bowl** (above).

A circle was cut from layers, which included double-sided Fast2Fuse. An inner circle approximately one-sixth of the radius and a 30° sector, A–B–C, were marked (see diagram, right). The shaded area was cut away, keeping the center circle intact for later. After quilting, the piece was joined along A–D and B–E and the outside edges finished with satin stitch.

The seam allowances, together with the 30° sector cut away, means that the small circle cut from the center is adequate to cover the hole at the center. The edges of the small circle were finished with satin stitch and the inner edge of the main piece was stitched in place, again using satin stitch.

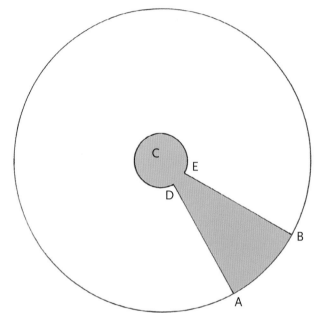

Dresden Bowl

1 Draw a circle about one-third the size of the finished bowl you wish to make and divide it into 12 sections, using the traditional Dresden Plate quilt block design for guidance.
2 Draw another circle around the Dresden Plate twice the size of the original. Thus, the radius of the new circle is at least 50 percent greater than the Dresden Plate's radius.
3 Draw the center lines of all 12 sectors, extending the lines to the circumference of the outer circle, A–B–C.
4 Copy one of the inner Dresden Plate sectors, including the central line, and cut it out (see diagram, right).
5 On this cut-out section draw a right-angled line, x–x, through the center of A–B, and cut the section into two pieces along this line (see diagram, far right). Discard the lower A part of this cut-out piece.

6 Lay the other (B) part of the section on to the outside edge of the larger circle, lining up the center lines, matching point B of the cut-out on to point C on the outer circle. The curved top lies outside the outer circle; the y points are on the circumference.
7 Draw lines from y to z to create a new, elongated section.

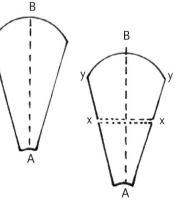

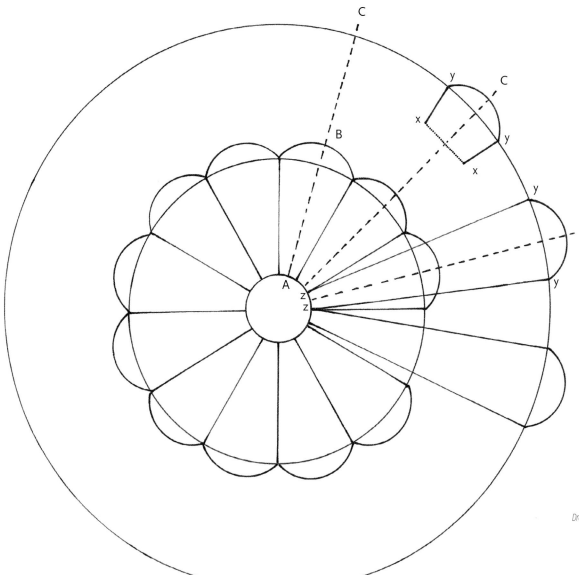

Below:
Dresden Bowl (C. June Barnes)
10" x 6" (25 x 15cm)

8 Repeat the last two steps on all 12 A–B lines.
Copy the new layout to another piece of paper,
discarding the original lines.

9 The result will be a flower-like shape with gaps
between the spurs of the plate.

10 Use this new design as a pattern to create a
layered, stiffened and stitched piece, quilting the
spurs and neatening the edges with satin stitch.

11 Join the outside corners of the curved spur tops
to one another at y.

12 The result is a cage-like bowl with attractive
scalloped edges.

If the piece is particularly large it may be
necessary to stiffen the edges of the spurs
with wire or boning.

Pieced Constructions

A wide range of three-dimensional geometric shapes can be made using textiles as a medium – they can be challenging but are very achievable! You need plenty of pins for some models, but generally most can be made with a little patience and some basic sewing skills (see page 13 for general assembly notes).

The shapes on the following pages can be made either angular with straight seams and edges or spherical by adding curves to the seams. Generally speaking, when adding curves to seams, the fewer pieces to the pattern the deeper the curve needs to be.

When making angular shapes, Pelmet Vilene or similar added to the layers gives a more rigid structure, which may not need stuffing for support, depending on its size.

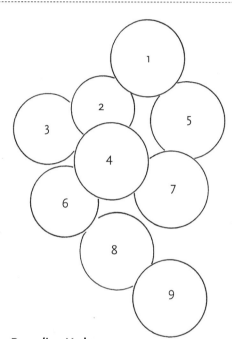

Rounding Up key

1 Truncated tetrahedron (see page 75)
   4 hexagons and 4 triangles

2 Cube (see page 69)
   6 squares

3 Tetrahedron (see page 70)
   4 triangles

4 4 segments (see page 81)

5 6 segments (see page 80)

6 Dodecahedron (see page 72)
   12 pentagons

7 Icosahedron (see page 72)
   20 triangles

8 Octahedron (see page 71)
   8 triangles

9 Cuboctahedron (see page 75)
   6 squares and 8 triangles

Platonic Solids

Opposite:
Rounding Up (C. June Barnes)
10—14" (25—35cm)
Nine constructed spherical shapes based on geometric solids. These are filled with toy stuffing.

Platonic solids are named after the Greek philosopher Plato and there are five of them – cube, tetrahedron, octahedron, icosahedron and dodecahedron. They are the only polyhedra whose faces are all exactly the same. For instance, a cube is a Platonic solid because all six of its faces are congruent squares. In addition to this they are the only three-dimensional solids that have the same number of faces meeting at each vertex. For example, three equilateral triangles meet at each vertex of a tetrahedron.

These solids can be combined to make more complex shapes.

Right:
Jewel Boxes (Lee Buchanan)
24" x 36" (60 x 90cm)
Polystyrene cubes in five sizes,
ranging from 2½" to 4" (7 to 10cm),
were covered with log-cabin blocks
on the top face.
The sides were reinforced with
laminated sheets to get a crisp
edge. The completed modules
were assembled and stuck to an
artist's canvas.

Cubes and cuboids
(6 squares)

Cubes are relatively easy to make and formed the foundation for Lee Buchanan's *Jewel Boxes* (left), which was made using solid cubes covered with pieced fabric panels and assembled to create interesting modular structures.

The pattern for a cube involves six sides that are assembled following the diagram below. This pattern can be adapted by having the central four squares in one piece.

Note: Adding registration marks at the points A, B, C, and D where the seams will meet at the "corners" of the cube will help when piecing the spherical version. Stay stitch along the stitching lines.

1 Make or cut the six square pieces (adding seam allowances). Lay these pieces out according to the diagram (left).
2 With right sides together, sew all the adjacent seams first. Do not stitch all the way to the edges. Leave the seam allowances unstitched, and secure the beginning and end of each seam with a few backstitches.
3 Trim away the batting from these seams if applicable.
4 Sew the side seams – A–D, C–A, C–B, and B–D – to one another. Start at the corners, pinning along the stitching lines and matching the corners snugly. As before, do not stitch into the seam allowance, and backstitch to secure at both ends. This is the same technique used for setting-in patches in patchwork, for example, adding squares to a six-point star. Trim batting away if applicable.
5 Finally, following the same method, stitch the top in place – but leave an opening for turning and stuffing. Trim the batting (if applicable) and turn right side out.
6 If this is a cover for a rigid block, such as a polystyrene cube, then the last three seams of the top will need to be attached by hand. If it is to cover a soft block such as foam, then you may be able to stitch one more seam first, finishing off by hand. If the shape is to be filled/stuffed then leave a section of the last seam open to allow turning and stuffing.

The spherical cube *Rounding Up 2* (see page 67) was assembled in the same way as the regular cube, but the sides were rounded as in the diagram shown left. The size of the square is roughly one-quarter of the circumference of the sphere you require.

Above right:
Woven Basket (Ingrid Press)
8" x 6" x 6" (20 x 15 x 15cm)

Tetrahedron (four triangles)

The spherical version in *Rounding Up 3* (see page 67) has sides equal to one-third of the circumference of the sphere made (see diagram, right). See also page 88 for instruction for using a single piece of fabric, where the seams at the apex were left unstitched.

1   Make four equilateral triangles and lay them out according to the diagram shown right.
2   First join the adjacent edges, stitching sides A, B, and C to the base. Carefully line up the corners – do not stitch all the way to the edges – leave the seam allowances unstitched. Secure the beginning and end of each seam with a few backstitches.
3   Next stitch the sides together – side A to side B, side B to side C, and side C to side A – carefully matching the points at the base corners and at the apex. Leave an opening in one seam for turning and stuffing.

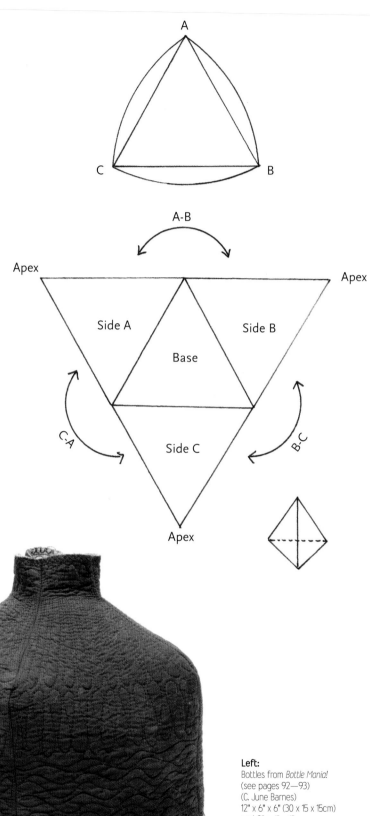

Left:
Bottles from *Bottle Mania!*
(see pages 92—93)
(C. June Barnes)
12" x 6" x 6" (30 x 15 x 15cm)
and 8" x 4" x 4"
(20 x 10 x 10cm)
The principles for making cubes (see page 69) and tetrahedrons were used for these structured bottles.

Octahedron (eight triangles)

Make eight equilateral triangles as for the tetrahedron and lay them out as in the diagram shown below. The sides of the triangles will be about one-quarter of the finished circumference.

First join all sides, laying them adjacent to one another, followed by the angled seams marked x, y, and z in the diagram. Continue to join subsequent seams that present themselves until all sides are stitched, but remember to leave an opening for turning and stuffing.

The spherical version is *Rounding Up 8* (see page 67).

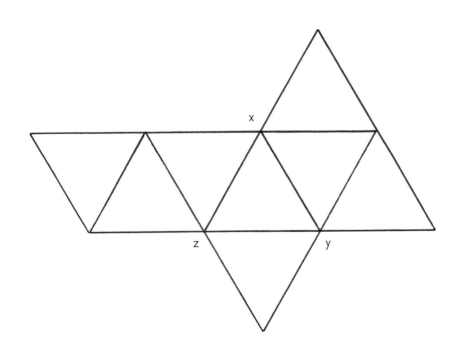

Above:
These octahedron forms can also be seen in *Rounding Up 8* (C. June Barnes) on page 67. 10—12" (25—30cm)

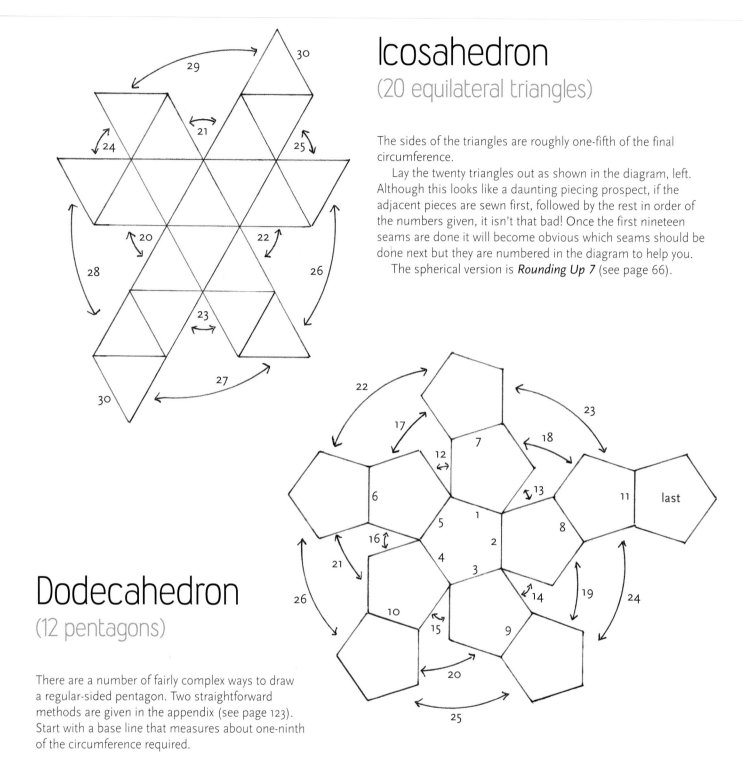

Icosahedron
(20 equilateral triangles)

The sides of the triangles are roughly one-fifth of the final circumference.

Lay the twenty triangles out as shown in the diagram, left. Although this looks like a daunting piecing prospect, if the adjacent pieces are sewn first, followed by the rest in order of the numbers given, it isn't that bad! Once the first nineteen seams are done it will become obvious which seams should be done next but they are numbered in the diagram to help you.

The spherical version is *Rounding Up 7* (see page 66).

Dodecahedron
(12 pentagons)

There are a number of fairly complex ways to draw a regular-sided pentagon. Two straightforward methods are given in the appendix (see page 123). Start with a base line that measures about one-ninth of the circumference required.

1   Lay the pentagons out according to the above diagram.
2   Work through the sequence, systematically following the diagram, first piecing the edges that are lying adjacent to one another – eleven in total.
3   Next, set in the seams between the inner pentagons 12 to 16, followed by the new seams from 17 to 21. After the last of the set-in seams, 22 to 26, have been completed you will be left with the last pentagon to be stitched in place.

The spherical version is *Rounding Up 6* (see page 67) and see also *Pure Fantasy: Dodecahedron* (opposite).

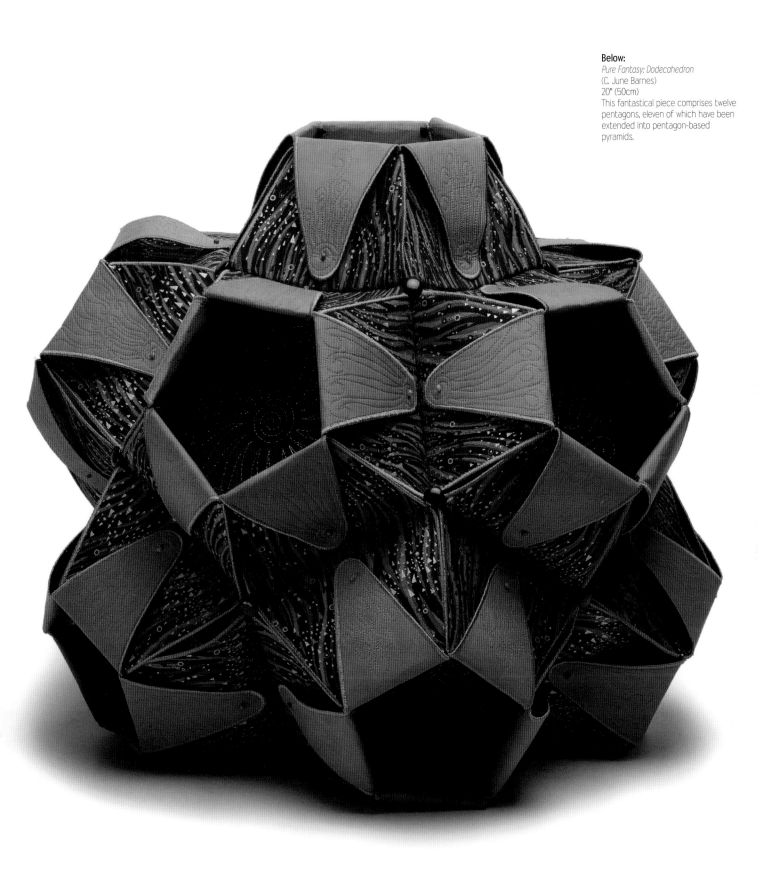

Below:
Pure Fantasy: Dodecahedron
(C. June Barnes)
20" (50cm)
This fantastical piece comprises twelve
pentagons, eleven of which have been
extended into pentagon-based
pyramids.

Archimedean Solids

Archimedean solids are distinct from Platonic solids because they are made of two or more regular polygons meeting at identical vertices (corners or intersections).

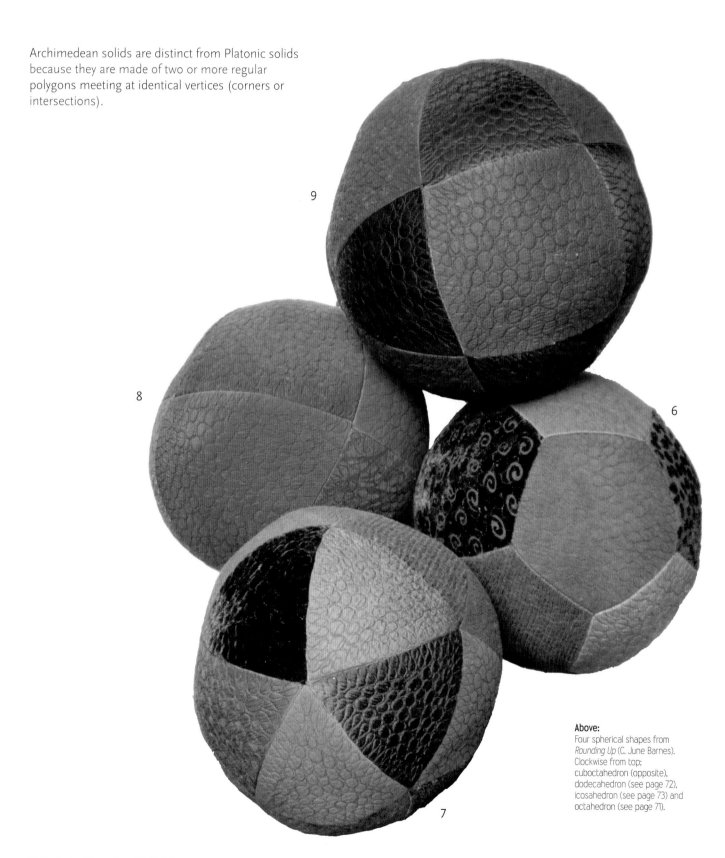

Above:
Four spherical shapes from *Rounding Up* (C. June Barnes). Clockwise from top; cuboctahedron (opposite), dodecahedron (see page 72), icosahedron (see page 73) and octahedron (see page 71).

Truncated tetrahedron
(four hexagons and four triangles)

The sides of the hexagons and triangles are just over one-seventh of the circumference.

1 Make clear registration marks at the six corners of the hexagons to assist with piecing.
2 Lay the pieces out according to the diagram, right.
3 First piece the edges that are lying adjacent to one another, 1 to 7.
4 Complete the seams following the numbered sequence until all pieces have been joined.

The spherical version is *Rounding Up 1* (see page 67).

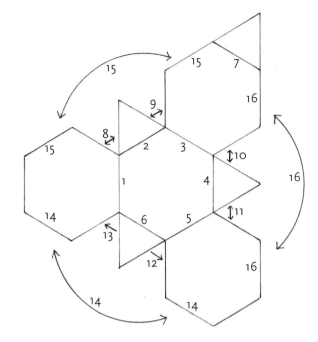

Note: As the hexagons can each be divided into six equilateral triangles equal in size to the four triangles, this pattern could be translated into twenty-eight equilateral triangles. This offers the opportunity to add more variety to the fabrics used and would also improve the spherical aspect. First construct the four hexagons using twenty-four of the triangles, and then complete the construction following the steps above.

Cuboctahedron
(six squares and eight triangles)

1 The sides of the six squares and eight equilateral triangles (based on the diagram shown left where the square A, B, C, D and triangle C, D, E are shown in one diagram) are about one-sixth of the circumference.
2 For the spherical version, make clear registration marks at the corners of the square to assist with piecing.
3 Lay the pieces out according to the diagram, left.
4 First piece the edges that are lying adjacent to one another (1 to 13) and then follow the numerical piecing order.

The spherical version is *Rounding Up 9* (see opposite and page 67).

Spherical Shapes and Orbs

A sphere is a solid bounded by a closed surface, every point of which is equidistant from a fixed point called the center.

Orbs can be either hollow as in *Pure Fantasy: Dodecahedron* (see page 73), solid (such as a covered polystyrene ball) or filled (stuffed) as in the components of *Rounding Up* (see page 67). The only way to get a true sphere with stitching is to use a foundation or framework to support the stitched layers. Pieced orbs from quilted sections are never perfect and so the term is used quite loosely! The calculations given for patterns in this section will produce spheres that are "near enough," and have the textile medium in mind. To make accurate patterns for perfect spheres you would need to use a Wulff grid or net and make far more complicated calculations.

How you go about constructing the components depends very much on the final article. Each unit of *Rounding Up* was pieced and then stuffed with toy filler. *Pure Fantasy: Dodecahedron* is a hollow construction that involved pieced sections with heavyweight stiffener in the pentagon sections. *Pure Fantasy: Bommyknocker* (opposite) is also hollow, supported by Lamitex added to the side sections.

These shapes are sometimes fiddly to stitch but are worth exploring. The patterns can be adapted to make toys, juggling balls and much more, but the intention here is to create components for installations, which are either single units, as in *Pure Fantasy: Dodecahedron* and *Pure Fantasy: Bommyknocker*, or a combination or repetition of smaller units – see *Rounding Up*, which is a collection of orbs, some of which were made by adapting Archimedean and Platonic solids featured on the previous pages.

Right:
Three four- and six-segmented bottles from *Bottle Mania!*, which is shown in full on pages 92—93
(C. June Barnes)
8—14" x 5—10"
(20—35 x 12—25cm)

Above:
Pure Fantasy: Bommyknocker
(C. June Barnes)
18" x 14" (45 x 35cm)
This five-section form was inspired
by a sea anemone. The colors and
patterning recall the features of
this amazing creature.

Piecing (cutting out components and assembling)

There are many piecing variations for sphere-like shapes, and depending on the size and number of faces the process can be time-consuming and complex. Larger units can be machine pieced, but it may be easier to work smaller pieces by hand (see also page 13). Generally speaking, the more pieces used the more spherical the result. Make a trial piece out of calico or similar before embarking on the main project. If any adjustments are needed the pattern can be tweaked to suit, saving time in the long run.

Two-piece orb

Here's how to draw the pattern for each part:

1 Draw a circle approximately the size of the sphere you want to make. You could use a circular object such as a plate as a template. Mark the diameter on the template (A–B). Extend this line about twice the length of A–B to one side of the circle (see diagrams, opposite).

2 Measure the diameter of A–B. Mark a spot C half of this diameter from B on the extended line.

3 Draw a second circle the same size as the first with C as the outside edge and the diameter lined up along the extended line to D.

4 Find the center of the line between B and C and mark this x. Draw a line E–F at right angles to B–C through x.

5 Join the two circles with arcs above and below B–C, forming a "neck" between the circles as in the diagram top right.

6 Mark the points G and H where the neck lines meet, E–F.

7 Add seam allowances and use this pattern make two pieces from contrasting fabrics, with the straight of grain running along A–D.

8 Make registration marks at A, B, G, and H – these will help when assembling the pieces. Snip the curves to make stitching them easier.

9 To assemble, line the pieces up at right angles to one another (see diagram bottom right), matching registration marks A to G and B to H. Pin thoroughly, sew carefully, leaving an opening for turning and stuffing. Refer to general assembly instructions on page 13.

Above:
Orb 1 (C. June Barnes)
8" x 8" x 4" (20 x 20 x 10cm)
Two-piece orb.

Note: Achieving a good round ball using this method is not very successful – you may need to adjust the distance between the circles depending on the fabric used. In the process of attempting to get a better ball using this method I discovered that placing the circles further apart and/or reducing the "neck" between the circles (C–D) resulted in a rectangular pod or capsule with rounded corners. See the capsules on page 99 for a variation on the use of this pattern shape and construction technique.

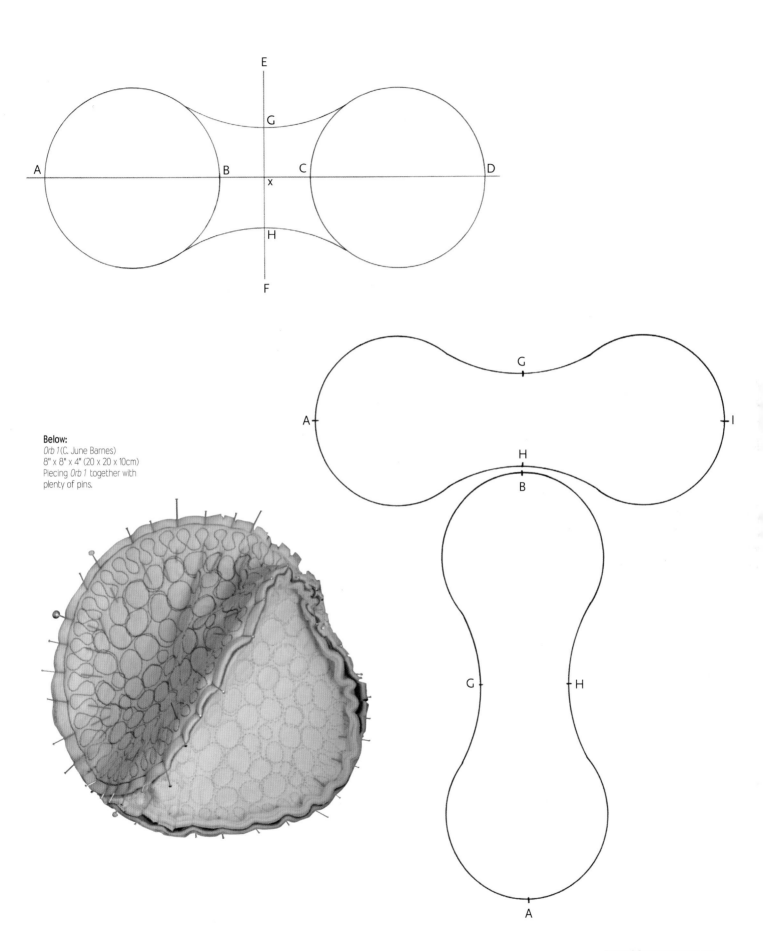

Below:
Orb 1 (C. June Barnes)
8" x 8" x 4" (20 x 20 x 10cm)
Piecing *Orb 1* together with
plenty of pins.

Six-piece orb

To draw the pattern for each segment, see diagram, right, and work as follows:

1 Draw a line A–B that is one-sixth of the circumference of the sphere required.
2 Using this line as a base construct a triangle on each side of A–B where the new sides are equal to one-quarter of the circumference of the sphere (ratio 3:2). Extend line A–B on either side of A and B.
3 Mark the apex points of these triangles, C and D.
4 Find the centers of A–C and A–D, and mark them x. Draw a right-angled line through these mid points, extending them so that they intersect at y. Using y as the center of a circle draw an arc that passes through A, D, and C.
5 Mark a point z along the extended line A–B so that B–z is equal to A–y. Using z as the center of a circle draw an arc that passes through C, B, and D.
6 Make six pieces using this pattern, with the straight of grain running from C to D.
7 Join the segments along the C–D arcs firstly into 2 sets of 3 (half spheres), and then join the two halves to one another, leaving a space in the last seam to allow for turning and stuffing.
8 Turn right side out and stuff as required.

See also **Rounding Up 4** (see page 67).

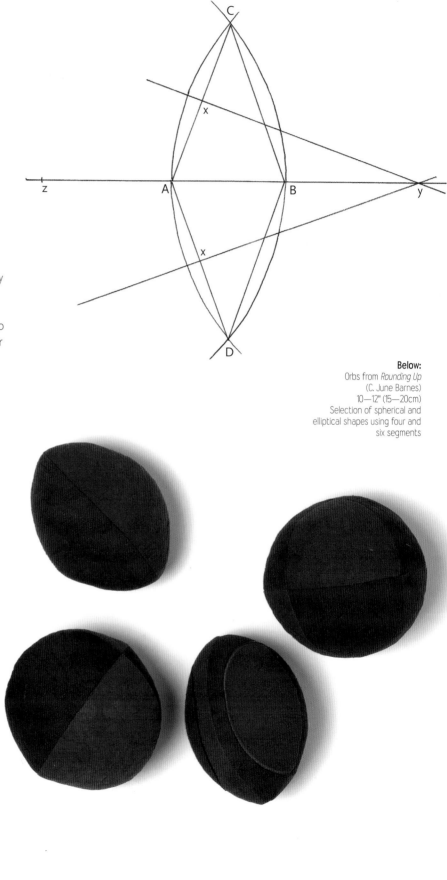

Below:
Orbs from *Rounding Up*
(C. June Barnes)
10—12" (15—20cm)
Selection of spherical and elliptical shapes using four and six segments

Here is another way to draw a segment pattern:

1 Draw a square in which the diagonal (A–B) is equal to about three-quarters the diameter of the sphere you wish to make.
2 Draw a triangle with 45° angles at A and B.
3 Where these lines meet is the third corner of the square – C.
4 Complete the square A, B, C, and D.
5 Using C and D as the center, scribe an arc running through A and B, on both sides of A–B (see diagram, right).

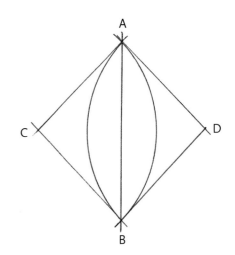

Four-piece orb

1 Make a pattern in the same way as described opposite, but make A–B one-quarter instead of one-sixth of the circumference (ratio 1:1).
2 Make four pieces using this pattern, with the straight of grain running from C to D.
3 Join the segments into two pairs along the C–D arcs and then join the two halves to one another leaving a space in the last seam to allow for turning and stuffing.
4 Turn right side out and stuff as required.

See also *Rounding Up 4* (see page 67).

Below:
Six- and four-segmented orbs
from *Rounding Up* (see page 67)
(C. June Barnes)
10—12" (20—30cm)

Elliptical shapes

The four- and six-piece orbs can be adapted to make either egg or pumpkin shapes by changing the ratio of the width and height of the pattern. Increasing the width of the segment pattern, while maintaining the length, will result in a "squashed" orb, while reducing it will result in a stretched orb similar to a rugby ball. Examples are shown opposite.

Pure Fantasy: Bommyknocker (on page 77) has five segments with a ratio of 1:2. This was based on the actual dimensions of a sea-anemone test case. The result was not very round; something that would be achieved by division into ten sections.

Crescents

Below:
Crescent Pods (C. June Barnes)
10" x 6" x 4" (25 x 15 x 10cm)
The seams are a feature of the
pod on the left, being placed
on the outside, while the more
usual arrangement of seams
inside is used for the pod on
the right. Notice how this makes
the left-hand pod look slimmer
and more angular.

The **vesica piscis** is the shape created by the area where two circles with the same radius overlap, where the center of each circle lies on the circumference of the other (see the diagram, opposite). The overlapping, fish-shaped area resembles a lens and as a symbol has been extensively used in Christian art. The **vesica** has many amazing properties. Two equilateral triangles can be drawn inside the **vesica** and a hexagon can be constructed, using it as a starting point (see Appendix, page 124, for further details). Further information about the **vesica** has been well explored by Robert Lawlor and Keith Critchlow (see Recommended Reading page 127).

The two outside, crescent-shaped sections can be joined to one another and stuffed to make a crescent-shaped capsule. Added dimension is achieved if the inner edges are stitched together and a gusset inserted to the outside curves, resembling an orange segment.

Perhaps the most pleasing shape is achieved when the inner lens section is inserted or stitched into the concave curves of the crescents, producing a three-dimensional, crescent-shaped capsule. This shape benefits from stiffening, making construction a little challenging. This depends on the scale used. *Ring Around the Moon* on page 84 comprises six crescent pods.

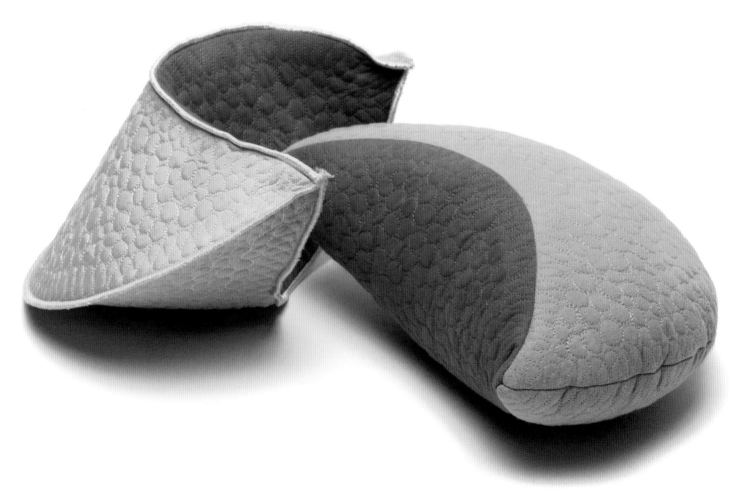

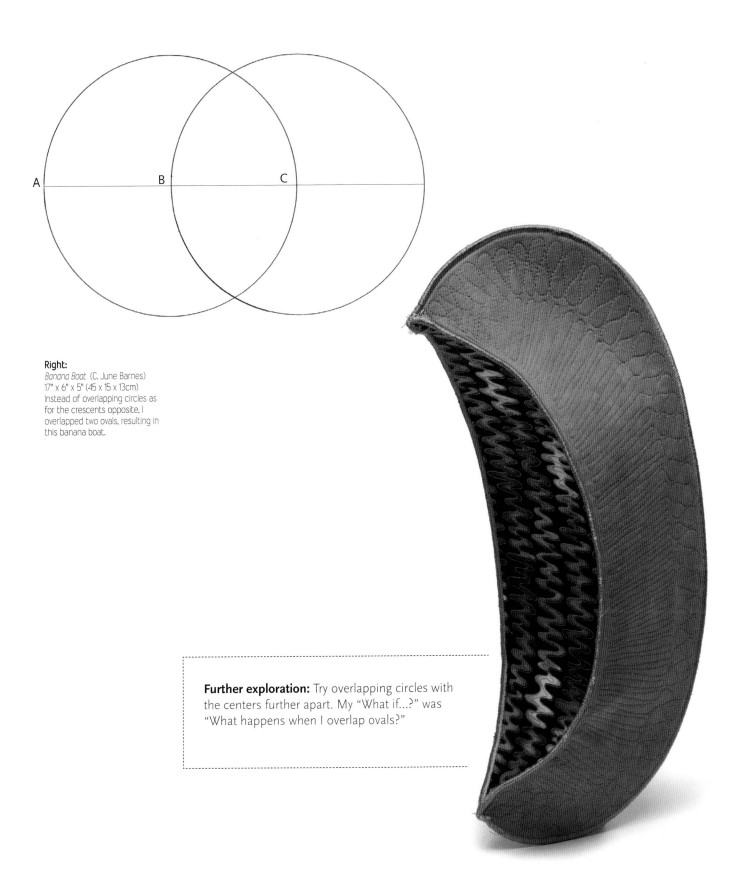

Right:
Banana Boat (C. June Barnes)
17" x 6" x 5" (45 x 15 x 13cm)
Instead of overlapping circles as
for the crescents opposite, I
overlapped two ovals, resulting in
this banana boat.

Further exploration: Try overlapping circles with
the centers further apart. My "What if...?" was
"What happens when I overlap ovals?"

A   B   C

Ring Around the Moon

Referring to *vesica piscis* (see diagram, page 83), make up a pattern for the **Crescent Pod**. The size of the inner circle of the project will be A–B and the circumference roughly 6 x B–C.

Draw the pattern parts for six pods on to lightweight backing fabric.

Make up the six inner crescent gussets (segment shaped), clearly marking the stitch line with stay stitching. These pieces deserve star treatment as they face outwards.

Next, make up the pairs of crescent pattern pieces in the same way. Although much of these pieces are hidden, it is still necessary to quilt the whole piece to get consistent reduction in size; the quilting that shows can be very effective and so color choice and quilting deserve careful consideration.

Once you have quilted the pieces, cut out laminating sheets or Pelmet Vilene to fit comfortably within the seam allowances. The pieces will not be the same size as the pattern parts – allowance has to be made for the effect of the quilting – and will not be stitched into the seams but added after assembly. It is worth numbering all pieces so that the correct stiffening can be matched to the correct section.

The batting in the seam allowance needs to be trimmed away; this is easiest to do before assembling the pieces. Cut away some of the batting from the seams, leaving enough for the satin stitch to bite into, but sufficient to avoid any batting showing through.

The following sequence of stitching is the least awkward.

To assemble each pod:

1. Firstly, stitch the gusset to the inner sides of the crescent pieces. The seams will be to the outside so stitch wrong sides together, using plenty of pins to assist! Do not snip the seam allowance of the crescent pieces excessively as they are exposed and need to be neatly over-sewn later. Leave the outer seam allowances at the points unstitched. Neaten the edges, and if you haven't yet done so, cut away some batting in the seams. Over-sew the edges with satin stitch – leaving the seam area for the outer crescent unstitched. It may require a few layers of satin stitch to end up with a smooth edge.

2. Next, attach the stiffening on to the inside of all three components – either ironing the Lamitex in place or using a glue gun. Trim these so that they lie within the stay stitching/seam allowance if necessary.

3. Close the outer seam of the crescent. Finish it off in the same way as the inner seams. I found small-toothed clamps/clips very useful when holding these edges together (see right). Machine stitching right to the point is not possible due to the restrictions of the presser foot so it will need to be finished by hand.

When all six pods have been made, arrange them into a circle with sharp ends together and secure them to one another either with stitch or glue.

All the parts for *Ring Around the Moon* were embellished with Shiva Paintstiks before they were assembled.

Right:
Ring Around the Moon, detail
(C. June Barnes)
When dealing with thick quilted layers,
it is often easier to use clamps to
secure the layers rather than pins.

Pyramids

A pyramid is technically a cone with a polygonal (many-sided) base. Connecting the base to an apex makes a pyramid. The diagram below shows a triangular-based pyramid. The following instructions make hollow, vessel-like shapes, but each can be stitched to the apex to create solid geometric shapes.

Triangular base
(tetrahedron)

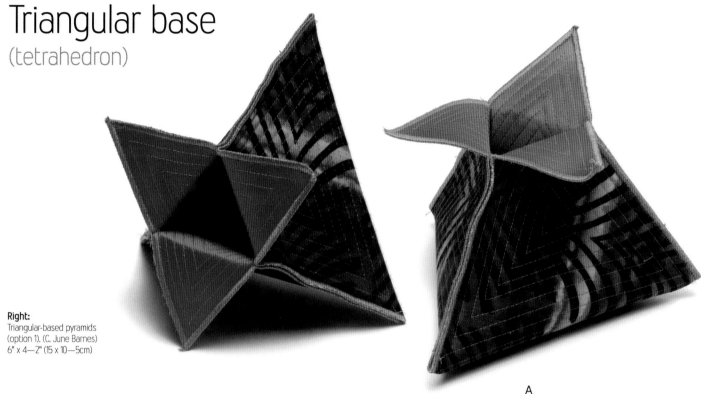

Right:
Triangular-based pyramids (option 1). (C. June Barnes)
6" x 4—2" (15 x 10—5cm)

Option 1

Referring to the diagram (right), start with an equilateral triangle which has sides roughly four times the finished height you require. To make the pattern:

1. Draw an equilateral triangle, A–B–C following the guidelines in the appendix (see page 123).
2. Mark the centers of each side of the triangle and mark them a, b, and c.
3. Draw a line between these points, creating a triangle within the triangle with sides a–b, b–c, and c–a.
4. Mark points that are half of the outside points x, y, and z.

To construct: finish all edges and join sides a–x to a–y; b–y to b–z, and c–z to c–x. Fold points outwards along lines x, y, and z.

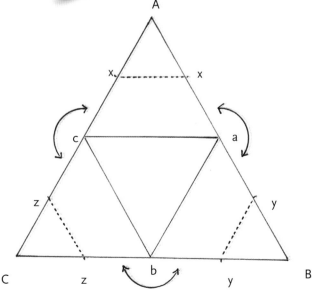

Option 2

Draw an equilateral triangle roughly the size of the base of the container you are making. Make the pattern (see diagram, right), following these steps:

1 Draw an equilateral triangle A–B–C following the guidelines in the appendix (see page 123).
2 Mark the centers of each side of the triangle and mark them a, b, and c.
3 Draw right-angled lines through a, b, and c and mark a point x on each about one-and-a-half times the length of sides A–B, B–C and C–A.
4 Draw three triangles A–B–x, B–C–x, and C–A–x.
5 Mark points * along the A–x, B–x, B–y, C–y, C–z, A–z sides at the finished height of the container.

To construct: finish all edges and join edges A–* B–* and C–*. Fold points towards the outside at *.

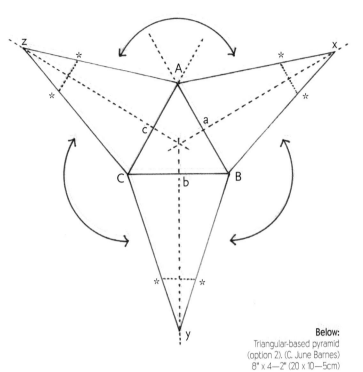

Below:
Triangular-based pyramid (option 2). (C. June Barnes)
8" x 4—2" (20 x 10—5cm)

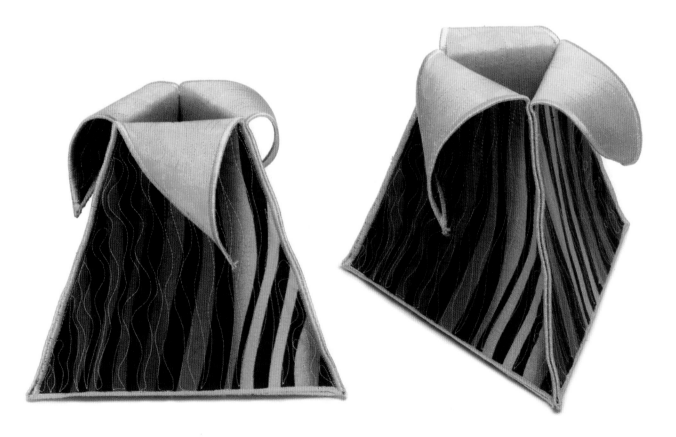

Square-based pyramid

The same construction technique can be adapted to using a square base. Referring to the diagram shown right, make the pattern:

1 Draw a square A–B–C–D, which is the size of the base required.
2 Draw right-angle lines through the centres of each side of the square a, b, c, and d.
3 Mark a point x on each of these lines equal to the height of the vessel planned, plus the turnover flap.
4 Draw four triangles A–x–B, B–x–C, C–x–D, and D–x–A.
5 Mark points ⁎ along both of the A–x, B–x, C–x, and D–x sides at the desired height of the box.

To construct: Finish all edges and join sides A–⁎, B–⁎, C–⁎, and D–⁎. Fold the points towards the outside at ⁎.

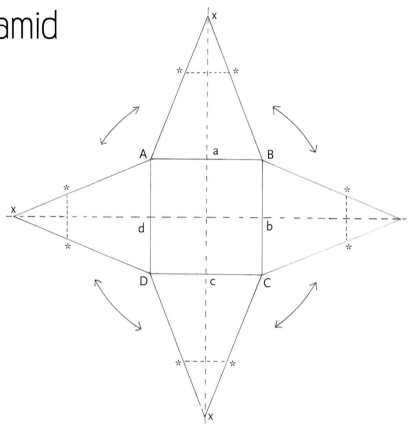

Left:
Pyramidal bottles from *Bottle Mania!*
(C. June Barnes)
With triangular base 5" x 5" x 5" x 10½" (13 x 13 x 13 x 27cm), shown left, and square base 5" x 5" x 5" x 12" (13 x 13 x 13 x 30cm), shown right.

Right:
Pure Fantasy: Dodecahedron, detail (C. June Barnes) Pyramids extended from the pentagonal surface of this piece.

Hexagonal base

Make a piece of work in the shape of a six-pointed star. Don't make it too small as it becomes very difficult to maneuver under the sewing machine. It may be necessary to piece this.
  To create the pattern (see diagram, below):

1　Draw a hexagon (refer to the appendix on page 124) the size of the base of the container.
2　Draw a right-angled line through the centre of each of the six sides and extend it outwards more than twice the length of the hexagon sides (lines A–B, B–C, C–D, D–E, E–F, and F–A).
3　Mark a point x along each of these six lines twice the length* of the base lines A–B, B–C, C–D, D–E, E–F, and F–A. (*Or the desired height of the container you wish to make.)
4　Draw triangles using the x points and the base lines (lines A–B, B–C, C–D, D–E, E–F and F–A), ending up with six triangles A–x–B, B–x–C, C–x–D, D–x–E, E–x–F, and F–x–A.
5　Mark the halfway points (y) on all long sides of these triangles and draw a line (y–y) across the triangle points. This is the height of the receptacle.

To construct: Finish all edges and join edges y–A to A–y; y–B to B–y; y–C to C–y, etc. Fold the x points towards the outside.

Above:
Hexagonal Pyramid (C. June Barnes)
9" x 7" (23 x 18cm)

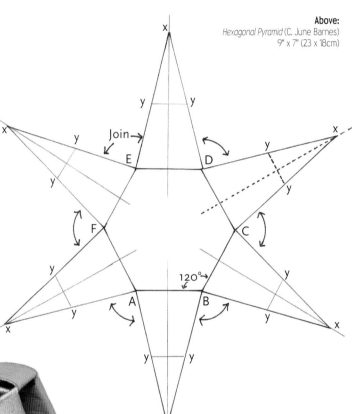

Experiment with different placements of x and y. Other variations can be achieved by changing the shape of the area above the y–y lines. These could be squared, rounded, or fringed.
  It is possible to build pyramids on any polygonal shape – the more sides the more complex the shape (see also Sandra Grusd's *Colourdance* on page 52).

Prisms

A prism has parallel sides with the same-shaped top and base, which also lie parallel to one another. It is described by the shape of its base. For instance, a rectangular prism has bases that are rectangles (cuboids), and a pentagonal prism has bases that are pentagons. (Circular and square or rectangular bases are covered elsewhere.)

Constructing a prism follows the same steps as used for the cube (see diagrams on page 69), but with adaptations to accommodate as many sides as are required. Some layout examples are given on these pages.

These constructions offer further opportunities when the "What if?" question is asked. What if you change the shape of the sides? Making the sides wider at the top, instead of them being parallel, and leaving the top off will result in a vase or bowl-like structure. Extending the sides further with parallel sides will make a deeper bowl. Adding yet another section will give you an urn. What if you combine three-dimensional shapes? See *Bottle Mania!* (see pages 92–93).

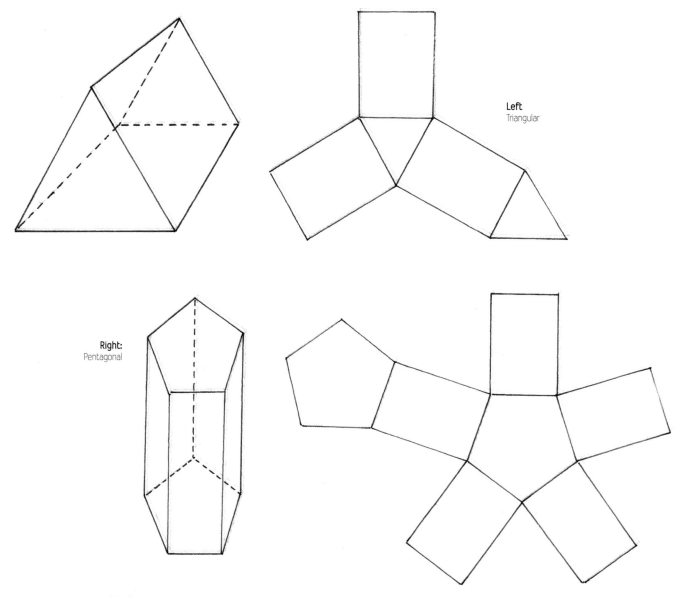

Left
Triangular

Right:
Pentagonal

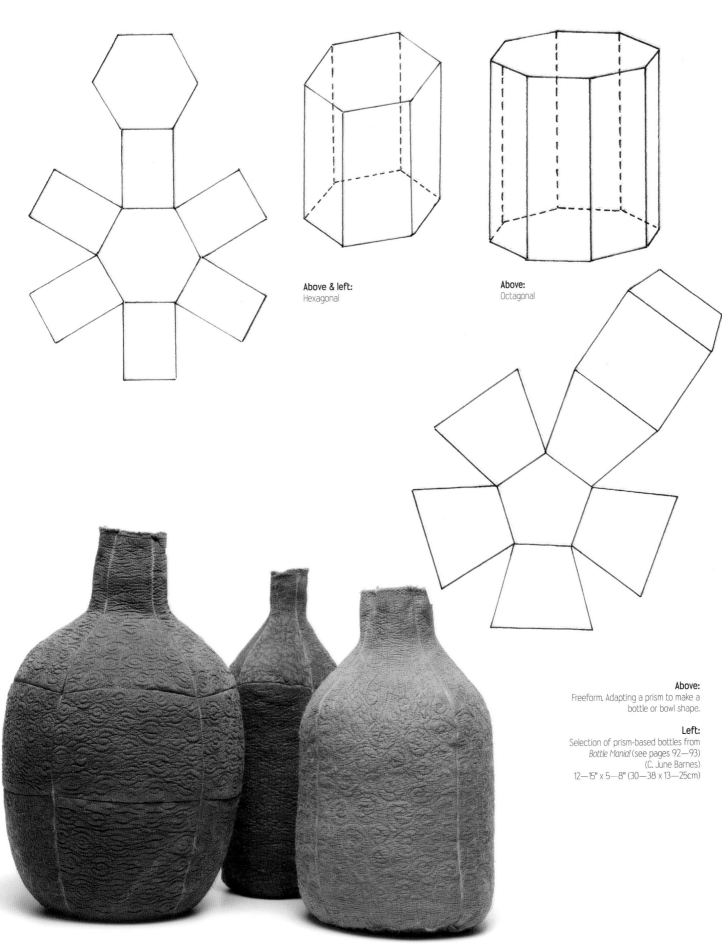

Above & left:
Hexagonal

Above:
Octagonal

Above:
Freeform. Adapting a prism to make a
bottle or bowl shape.

Left:
Selection of prism-based bottles from
Bottle Mania! (see pages 92—93)
(C. June Barnes)
12—15" x 5—8" (30—38 x 13—25cm)

Below:
Bottle Mania! (C. June Barnes)
18—8" x 6—10" (45—20 x 15—25cm)
An array of bottle shapes based on
the piecing instructions explored on
the previous pages and filled with
vermiculite, which is supportive
without being too heavy.

Cylinders

A cylinder is a prism with a circular base (see *Prisms*, pages 90–91). A cylinder is called a right cylinder if it is straight – its cross-sections lie directly on top of each other; otherwise, the cylinder is said to be oblique, as with the cones on page 62. Inger Milburn's *Zip Tree* (see page 111) is an example of a right cylinder. It is supported by a 7' 2" (220cm) long cardboard roll, which in turn is supported by a heavy-duty square of metal with a 2ft (60cm) long, 6" (15cm) diameter cylinder welded to it.

Reducing the size of the circular planes and stacking these on top of one another in gradation – large to small – results in a cone, as in *Aspirations* (see page 34).

These structures offer many possibilities for textiles. If it is necessary for them to be hollow, for a container or lamp for example, the textile components would need to be either stiffened sufficiently to stand on their own, or supported by a framework. If they do not need to be hollow they could be attached to a solid base made of foam or polystyrene. The size of the finished project will largely dictate what can be used. Some bottles in the *Bottle Mania!* range are cylindrical – see the image on page 91.

My *Empty Vessel* (see page 96) is a hollow cylinder, which could be used as a decorative light installation. The surface is made of sixty small, individual "puff balls" or "doughnuts" linked to one another. These have been attached to a framework of stainless steel, the ends of which have been drilled into a heavy base.

While working with pinwheels it struck me that it would be interesting to use these at the top of a container. I then became aware of the work of the ceramicist Erin Jones, and a combination of these factors inspired *Topping Up* (opposite), a collection of three cylinders with the top edges divided into two, three and four sections tied in various ways.

Right:
Pleated Vessels (Ingrid Press)
8" x 3" (20 x 7cm)

Below:
Topping Up (C. June Barnes)
14" x 3" (36 x 8cm)
The fabric used for these cylinders
was dyed by Leslie Morgan.

Capsules

Some of the geometric shapes explored lend themselves to creating capsules or pods when duplicated and joined to one another. Cones, especially those with a low apex, would make good flying-saucer-like shapes.

The doughnuts technique used on page 19 was adapted to make the individual modules, which make up *Empty Vessel* (opposite). On a larger scale they could be used to make even bigger capsules.

Empty Vessel

Circles about twice the size of the required capsule were drawn in pairs. It is impossible to make a firm suggestion for the size of the circles because the rate of shrinkage varies according to numerous conditions, such as water temperature and materials used. It is a matter of trial and error as there are so many variables involved.

Thin batting was used at the back of the circles (see step 4 on page 19), instead of viscose-wool felt or fabric. After the work was washed and dried the circles were cut out along the outside edge. These units were then glued to pieces of covered Pelmet Vilene at the back, forming a capsule that looks a little like a half doughnut. Two half doughnuts could be attached to one another to create a full, double-sided doughnut. If the scale was larger it may be necessary to include a layer of stiffener between the two sections for support.

Empty Vessel was made using 60 single-sided or half doughnuts attached to covered Pelmet Vilene and suspended on a framework.

Left:
Empty Vessel (C. June Barnes)
21" x 12" (54 x 30cm)

Above right:
Single "half doughnut" unit.
3½" x 2in" (9 x 5cm)

D-Forms — capsules with a difference

Some years ago I bought a small mood light, which has the most pleasing twisted, oval shape. I recently came across the work of Tony Wills, a product designer and partner in Wills Watson+Associates (wills-watson.co.uk), who discovered D-Form geometry. His concept helped to explain how I might achieve a similar shape. This is an exciting technique, which is so simple and yet so effective.

By joining the edges of two flat shapes that have the same perimeter length, you can create the three-dimensional forms that he named D-Forms. As Tony Willis points out, "strictly speaking D-Forms are made using unstretched, developable surfaces and have "single point curvature." If you can smoothly cover a surface with paper without any tears or wrinkles, it is developable. For example, a cone is developable and has single point curvature whilst a sphere is not developable and has a bicurvature surface." As I use fabric, which has some stretch to it, the capsules produced are therefore not true D-Forms but pods or capsules with D-Form-like properties.

While I was making an orb from two parts as used for a tennis ball I stumbled across a construction, which is essentially a D-Form. It wasn't until later, when I got a copy of the publication *D-Forms* by John Sharp (see Recommended Reading, page 127) and learnt of Tony Wills's D-Forms that the penny dropped and I realized that I had accidentally made something very similar.

The possibilities of these constructions are endless and well worth exploring. John Sharp's book works primarily with models made of card, explaining the concept clearly and offering many variations to explore. Working the models using textiles is very exciting and involves some adaptation, especially with the folds necessary to assist in some combinations of shapes. Because of the flexibility of textiles, using them to make these structures is perhaps easier than using card.

The essential thing to remember is that the perimeters of the two shapes you join need to be equal. Adding a stiffener to the layers enables the piece to have a rigidity that supports the shape, but they can alternatively be stuffed.

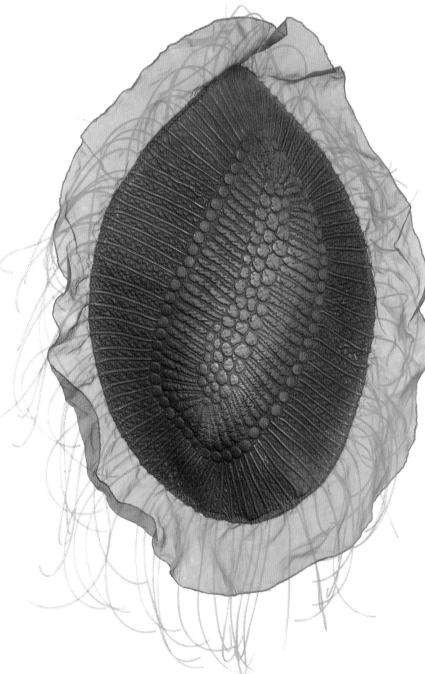

Left:
Pure Fantasy: D-Formity
(C. June Barnes)
4" x 6" x 5" (10 x 24 x 13cm)

Joining identical shapes to one another

Two identical asymmetrical shapes are used to make a D-Form.

For *Peanut* (above) I used the sphere produced in *Orb 1* on page 78 as a starting point. I redrew the pattern with the two circles touching one another as shown in the diagram below left. What I learnt from Tony Wills and John Sharp was that if, instead of assembling the pieces at right angles to one another as on page 79 (to be referred to as a right-angled pod), the alignment of the same pieces is offset one against the other

before they are stitched together, then a very different shape is made. Imagine a peanut-shaped clock face where 12 and 6 are at A and B (see diagram below right). Start by matching the 12 o'clock point on one piece to the 1 o'clock point on the other and complete the seam all the way around (to be referred to as an off-set pod) (shown above). Starting at different initial joining points of the same pair of shapes will result in an array of three-dimensional shapes.

Above:
Peanut (C. June Barnes)
12" x 4—5" (30 x 12—15cm)
An off-set pod based on a two-piece sphere pattern.

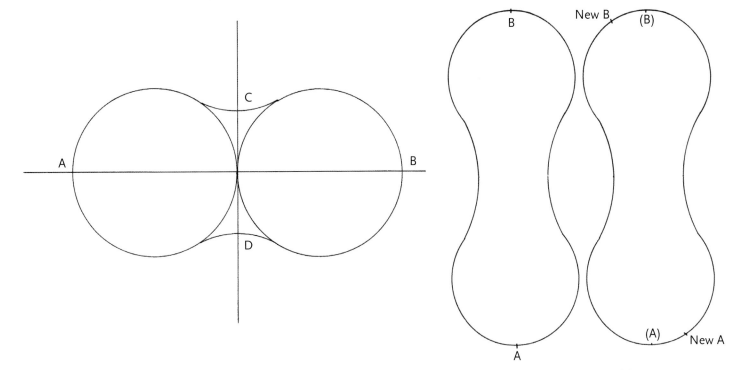

Any identical shapes other than a pair of circles can be used. These could be precisely constructed geometric shapes or drawn freehand, as long as the perimeters are the same and the sides are generally convex (bowing outwards rather than inwards or straight). Try tying the ends of a piece of cord into a loop and arranging it into a random shape on a piece of paper to create a template. *Pear Shaped* (right) was made using two identical pear shapes drawn freehand.

Right:
Pear Shaped (C. June Barnes)
12" x 5—2" (25 x 12—5cm)
Off-set pear shapes.

Far right top:
Pods 3 & 4 (C. June Barnes)
6" x 5" x 5" (15 x 15 x 13cm)
Vesica piscis, right-angled
and off-set.

Far right bottom:
Pods 5 & 6 (C. June Barnes)
6" x 6" x 5" (15 x 15 x 13cm)
Triangles, right-angled and off-set.

Try using two oval shapes (see the appendix, page 124, for instructions on drawing an oval or ellipse), with both the major and minor axis marked on the perimeter, or oval shapes drawn freehand and duplicated as in *Pure Fantasy: D-Formity* on page 98. *Pods 3 and 4* (above) were made using the middle section of the diagram *Vesica Piscis* on page 83. *Pod 4* is similar to a tetrahedron. To construct "pods" or capsules using shapes with sharp points in the edges, stitch from point to point separately, snipping the straighter edge on the opposite side at the points before moving on to the next section. Rounding off the points will give a different look to these pods.

The corners of triangles (*Pods 5 and 6*, below), oblongs and other shapes can be rounded off to make piecing easier, but can be assembled as they are, with a little application.

Joining different shapes to one another

Joined shapes can be totally different from one another. There are two options for assembling the parts:

- They can be stitched to one another right sides together, leaving an unstitched space to enable turning the capsule right side out.
- They can be stitched together with the seam allowance on the outside of the capsule, as turning stiffened projects inside out once assembled is not always possible.

In both cases registration marks help when lining the pieces up. One or other of the pieces, or indeed both, could be pieced, appliquéd or embellished before assembling.

Square to a circle

Joining a square to a circle is one of the D-form shapes discovered by Tony Willis. He named it a "squaricle." To do this, divide the circumference of a circle by four and make a square using that measurement. It is necessary to make folds or creases in the circle so that it adapts its shape to that of the square.

To engineer this I cut a matching circle of laminating sheet into quarters and ironed it to the underside of the circle after it had been quilted. Pelmet Vilene or similar would also work. The cut or creased edges were lined up with the corners of the square.

John Sharp and others discovered several alternative ways of creasing the circle. These are shown in John Sharp's book, *D-Forms* (see Recommended Reading, page 127). The inclusion of the laminating sheet made turning the pod impossible, and so the seams were stitched with the seams to the outside and the edges finished with satin stitch. See also **Upper Reaches** (right) which is a series of pods made of decreasing circles and squares stitched to one another in this way. The edges were bound rather than over-sewn.

Not all combinations are particularly striking or interesting. Those worth trying are an oblong stitched to a square, an expanded circle to an oblong and a triangle to a square or circle.

Right:
Square to Circle (C. June Barnes)
10" x 10" x 4" (25 x 25 x 10cm)

Featured Artists

Quilt artists and quiltmakers using dimension are still rather thin on the ground, but their numbers are growing. Many more embroiderers and textile artists already work with dimension. The introduction of categories such as that of Quilt Creations at the Festival of Quilts in Birmingham has encouraged this expansion.

Those featured on the following pages are some of the British quilters and textile artists who have generously shared thoughts in connection with their explorations into the world of three dimensions.

Left:
Upper Reaches (C. June Barnes)
43" x 14—9" (110 x 35—22cm)
The "roof" sections of *Upper Reaches* are circles of varying sizes stitched to squares with the same perimeter size.

Collective Purple

(Christine Chester, Dee Chester, Edwina Lelliot,
Sarah Morison, Sally Skaife, and Gill Streeter)

Having previously completed several projects that resulted in hangings made up of sections sewn by individual members, Collective Purple decided to do a project that we could easily dismantle into individual sections for each member to take home. Having explored one- and two-sided projects, the next step was to move from two into three dimensions, providing us all with a challenge. As several of the group had some experience with three-dimensional textile work it was an exciting prospect rather than a daunting one!

We were inspired by an article in a 2007 issue of **Embroidery Magazine** about Kay Khan who makes heavily stitched vessels with quite complex forms. We created a series of vessels that jigsawed together to make a whole. There followed a lot of design decisions that had to be made, which were extra to those we were used to making and which were generated by working with that third dimension.

The first decision we took was that the base of each vessel would be rectangular as we knew this could be easily measured and make the jigsaw stable. Two faces would be flat, while the jigsawing sides could take any form. Each of us drew one jigsaw edge of our "vase" and then brought them together and worked out the order of the edges and heights to give balance and interest across the piece.

Above:
Sunburst Vase, back
(Collective Purple)
42" x 15" x 5" (107 x 38 x 13cm)

Below:
Sunburst Vase, front
(Collective Purple)
42" x 15" x 5" (107 x 38 x 13cm)

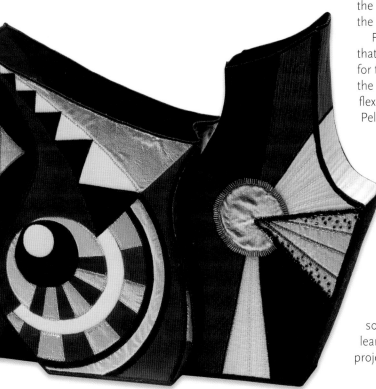

Our design theme was to be Art Deco, which gave us a palette of colors to work with, and the sunburst theme came from one member who made a design to run across the front face of all the vases. The reverse of the vessels would then be individual sunbursts and as they were to be different depths as well as heights; this would give us a staggered back to the set.

Of course, our design was three-dimensional and so the sides had to be considered as an integral part of the design of the vases. Not only would they eventually be individual pieces in our homes, but together there was an uneven face, which revealed some of the sides in the design of the whole piece. We opted to continue the sunburst rays around the jigsaw edge.

For the practical expression of our idea, we needed materials that would do two different jobs. We investigated Pelmet Vilene for the rigid flat planes, but considered this too stiff for some of the intricate jigsaw edges required. We used acrylic felt for these flexible sides, knowing that both quilting, and the support of the Pelmet Vilene sides, would help keep the felt in shape.

The problem that caused us the most difficulty was how to join the sides of the vase together, given the complexity of forms we had chosen. After various samplings of binding and insertion stitches, we settled on zigzagging a small cord all around the edge, which could then be used to lace the sides together with a simple lacing stitch.

Our vases did have another dimension of course: the inside. The sharpness of the Art Deco theme meant that we wanted to keep the inside of the vessels equally clean, so we simply bonded the lining on after all the stitching had been completed but before satin stitching the edges.

We are all delighted with the finished project. There were some interesting problems to solve along the way and we learned a lot about working in three dimensions. Our next project is moving on with this theme.

Audrey Critchley

I visited Bathurst Island, an Aboriginal Tiwi settlement, a 45-minute flight from Darwin, where I saw at first hand *tali pukamani* poles (grave posts) erected around the graves. Also, in the Art Gallery of New South Wales in Sydney there is a wonderful collection of grave posts, which I often draw on my visits to Australia.

The installation consists of five celebration poles based on the aboriginal posts. The three long printed cloths hanging behind the posts have been dyed, printed and stitched to represent the turquoise sea of Australia. The posts are different sizes, both in height, from 6'–6' 9" (183–207cm), and circumference, 11" to 21" (29–53cm).

I made personal cloths to wrap around cardboard cylinders. Some were hand embroidered, while for others I used batik, paint, and print. Some cloths were bright, others muted. I wanted to convey a feeling of height and depth to the piece. Simple running stitch gave me endless patterns. The squiggly lines are based on the marks made by a parasitic worm under the bark of a gum tree. Its wanderings look like graffiti. I think of these lines as pathways.

Making the grave posts became a challenge. I had to think how to present them upright. Eventually I used cardboard tubes that are used to wrap carpets around, which fortunately come in different diameters and lengths.

The square base to display them on presented problems as I did not want them to be exactly upright. My husband helped me fix angled pieces of steel to the base, which the cardboard tubes could slip over, thus enabling us to achieve the variations in positions that I wanted.

Below:
Aboriginal *Tali pukamani*, or prayer posts.

Left and above:
Grave Posts, with detail
(Audrey Critchley)
72—78" x 11—21"
(183—207 x 29—53cm)
Carpet tubes are used to support
the fabric covers, which are then
secured to the base.

Pat Deacon

I have always regarded quiltmaking as a type of construction. Building a quilt made of squares is similar to building a brick wall, with the glorious exception of being able to move into the world of color and curve. I have spent my life making objects from wood and brick as well as fabric, so it is probably unsurprising that once captivated by the quilting world many of my quilts became structures rather than traditionally styled comforters.

When embarking on a quilt-related dimensional structure the problems usually relate to presentation, given that many quilt shows demand a sleeve on the back of the quilt for hanging purposes.

I designed *Fantasy Quilt* (left) as a large quilt made from nineteen "blades." The linkage of these blades is a bolt through the bottom of each blade, as with all fans. The only accommodation needed was to reduce the thickness by cutting back the batting where the blades overlapped. The main problem was always the method of hanging. Creating a sleeve on a fan-shaped quilt without the top flopping forward was not easy. Carbon-fiber rods in a hang-gliding shop were the solution! A length of rod was threaded through small rouleau loops on the tip of each blade and anchored in a small fabric pocket at each end. Carbon-fiber rods are strong and flexible and so push the blades outwards – perfect to hold curved edges in place.

Making *Fantasy Quilt* was the catalyst that set me on the quilt construction road. Weaving is a useful technique to use when wishing to create dimension. *All Squared Up* (opposite) is a simple piece of weaving with curved woven lines. Curves always add a sense of movement to any design. The weaving allows you to move into three dimensions because once the strips have been woven they can be manipulated into a bowl-like shape. When all the edges are stitched together the manipulations do not move. The quilt was mounted on to a frame with central struts supporting a plastic bowl covered with batting, which in turn supported the three-dimensional weaving. This enabled hanging the piece without a sagging middle.

My most ambitious project to date has been the production of *Mood Swing* (left) Unusually the basic design consisted of straight lines. The main challenge was to produce a "quilt" made of tessellating diamonds, each of which could be rotated to give a variety of color choices.

The first structural requirement was for each diamond to be firm. This was achieved by using foam-board instead of batting. I could then cut out a central core to allow each diamond to be threaded on to a steel rod. I cut a groove around the perimeter in order to tuck in the seams. The positioning of each diamond on the foam-board was crucial as the overall pattern had to line up, whichever side of the diamond was displayed.

The second structural requirement was to make a frame to hold the diamonds in place while still allowing them to be rotated. The main frame was held away from the wall by using four short legs with two picture hooks on the top two legs, which hook onto screws in the wall.

As a construction this piece worked very well. The problem was persuading both judges and spectators to interact with the piece and move the diamonds around to create different color combinations. I suppose that when normal quilting boundaries are pushed, it will take time for everyone else to catch up, but what fun it is dreaming up new ways in which the world of quilting can be pushed towards the world of three dimensions.

When embarking on these projects I only have a vague idea of what I am trying to create. When something hasn't been done before it's rarely impossible; it just needs a bit of problem-solving. It's very much a matter of taking one step, solving the problem, taking the next step and "sew on!"

Opposite (top):
Fantasy Quilt, detail (Pat Deacon, photographed by Pat Deacon) 79" x 55" x 4" (200 x 140 x 10cm)

Opposite (bottom):
Mood Swing, detail (Pat Deacon photographed by Pat Deacon) 29" x 52" (74 x 130cm)

Below:
All Squared Up (Pat Deacon photographed by Pat Deacon) 27" x 27" x 6" (69 x 69 x 15cm)

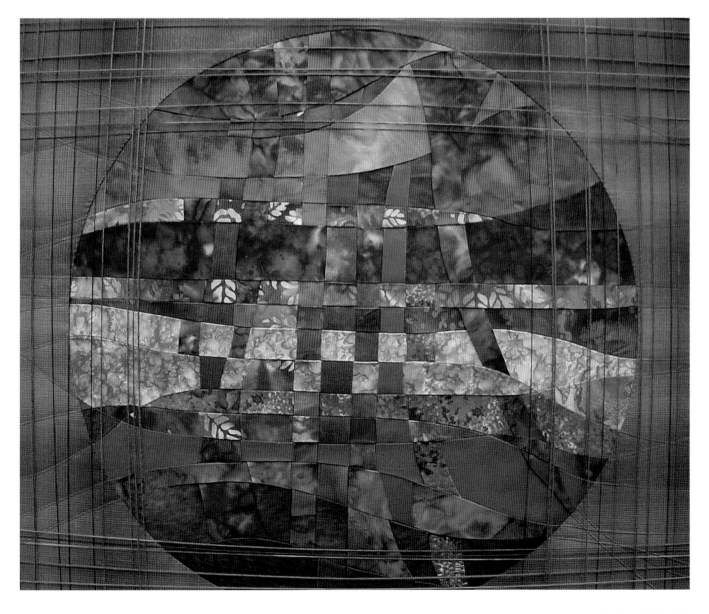

Inger Milburn

My textile work forms a commentary on subjects that catch my attention or preoccupy me as I go along. As well as other interests, this includes the fabrics and sewing techniques themselves. In a craft such as patchwork and quilting the materials are not just a means to an end; they have an intrinsic interest to be contemplated as part of the process of designing and making. When you make a bed-quilt, the way the finished product looks on the actual bed is of prime importance. The size, the distribution of pattern and color and the texture should all contribute to making it an inviting bed-cover. Once you move the quilt from the horizontal to the vertical by hanging it on a wall, the rules change. Although there is a tendency to regard a wall-hanging as a substitute for a framed painting and therefore to keep it square and flat, there is no need to submit to such restrictions. In fact, it can actually move right off the wall and be any shape you choose.

When I first started making my own designs, I spent a great deal of time on preparatory drawings and samples. With experience this has become less important, but the main reason for abandoning this way of working is the lack of spontaneity it allows. There is a contradiction between the wish to be spontaneous and the fact that quilt-making is intrinsically a slow business. This is something I am trying to overcome. In everything I make, I hope to combine something of the original flash of inspiration, as it occurred to me, with the demands of the process involved in realizing it, at the same time allowing the materials to dictate changes as the work progresses. This is especially the case with three-dimensional work, where technical considerations can easily come to dominate and where there are few precedents.

It has been necessary to find a variety of ways to support three-dimensional pieces in order to display them, ranging from wooden supports to specially designed supports made to measure. For *Orange Bowl* (left) which is made from two shallow curved shapes, I used a length of strimmer wire encased in the binding of each half, tensioned by a bead glued to the ends of the wire. The idea for this bowl came from the study of a fresh pine cone with its tightly overlapping scales. My original intention was to use a number of overlapping scales made from scraps of fabric in a controlled color range, but I ended up simplifying this to just two large scales and introduced a black and white accent for the orange.

Several of my free-standing pieces rely on a stand made specially to support them: a heavy-duty square of metal with a 2' (60cm) long, 6" (15cm) diameter cylinder welded to it. This supports my *Zip Tree* (opposite), which has zips used in different ways. A 7' 2" (220cm) long cardboard roll, which fits snugly on the stand, is covered by a spiraling pieced and quilted fabric length, held in place by one long zip. This covering is interrupted at intervals by short, vertically placed zips, which open to reveal a red, quilted lining with red drops spilling out from each opening.

Another piece, *Looking Through* (see page 39), uses the same support. In this case, a long double-sided piece can be twisted and turned in a number of ways and then locked in place by a rod threaded through lops and circular holes along the edges. I like to make things that are colorful, but with an edge of ambiguity.

Below:

Orange Bowl (Inger Milburn, photographed by Inger Milburn) 18" x 8—15" (45 x 20—38cm)

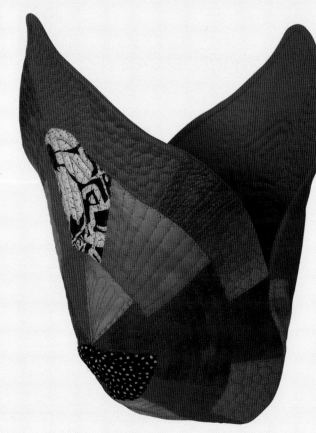

Below:
Empty Vessel (Inger Milburn,
photographed by Inger Milburn)
20" x 9—12" (50 x 23—30cm)

Right:
Zip Tree (Inger Milburn,
photographed by Ray Vine)
88" x 8" (225 x 20cm)

Eva Thomas

A driving force for making textile art is the enormous scope for innovation and variety in design, materials to choose from, and construction techniques. Add the possibility of working multi-dimensionally and even more exciting possibilities emerge.

Peace Pebbles

To pick up and hold smooth pebbles eroded into their present shape by the sea can be a soothing and peaceful experience while walking on a beach.

The longing for peace between nations was the design source for **Peace Pebbles** (see below). Each pebble has two sides and is stuffed with batting. The pebbles resemble the shapes and forms of natural pebbles. Seaweed-green yarn surrounds each pebble. Cut-back appliqué reveals a large peace symbol shape. One pebble is embellished using glass beads with the word PAX, meaning peace in Latin. The pebbles are stitched on to a fabric that reflects light in a similar way to the surface of water. The larger pebbles are 2" (5cm) high. The whole piece is displayed on a low plinth with the viewer peering down on the pebbles as if standing on the water's edge.

The pebbles were not difficult to construct in three dimensions. I noticed while the project gradually grew with pebbles being joined together, that it gave me more satisfaction, an extra joy, which would not have been there if I had made the piece in just two dimensions. To view the pebbles in the sunlight with natural shadows made the piece come alive like pebbles in nature.

Peace Pebbles (Eva Thomas, photographed by Eva Thomas)
48" x 2" (120 x 5cm)

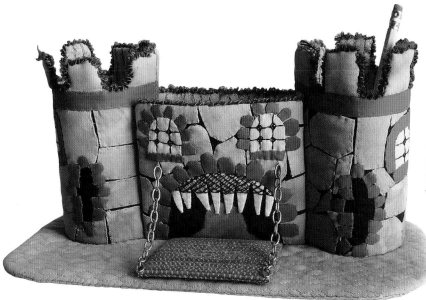

The Castle — A desk tidy

I sought to develop a unique desk tidy, which, while still being functional, had a theme. I settled for a medieval castle design following several visits exploring Bodiam Castle with its moat.

The central feature of the desk tidy is the drawbridge that can be lifted up. The entrance and portcullis resemble a wide-open mouth with sharp teeth. The top-floor windows look like eyes above the mouth. The walls and towers have been machine appliquéd on to a background fabric. The pieces were supported by cardboard and handstitched together. The broad base resembling the moat adds stability. It is large enough to store a varied selection of pencils, paintbrushes, scissors, and a ruler. Rubbers and paper clips rest on the moat.

The Love Can — A watering can

Janis Parle, a co-member of the textile art group Blue Tulips, set a challenge for each of us in the group to make a watering can using our own design and construction technique. We were encouraged to decorate the can in our own individual style.

My watering can is made out of heavyweight Vilene and is purely ornamental. Instead of containing water I imagine my can contains Love Potion, which is poured out of the spout as and when required. The text on label attached to the handle says:

Mental Health Warning:
Contains
LOVE POTION
HIGHLY ADDICTIVE
Go on, be reckless, use it often!

The can has been painted green and rusty brown using acrylic paint. I designed and painted heart shapes on cartridge paper using Koh-I-Noor and Aztec gold paint. The heart shapes were machine stitched to the Vilene. Black Fuse FX covers the entire surface, adding a rustic, weathered look. The can is embellished with small glass beads and red heart-shaped beads.

The parts of the can have been handstitched together using invisible monofilament thread. It was a bit awkward to assemble, especially stitching the spout to the main part. It is more fun in three dimensions as it's possible to lift up the can and shower someone with heaps of love, which would not have been possible if it had been constructed in two dimensions.

Above left:
The Castle (Eva Thomas, photographed by Eva Thomas) 12" x 6" x 156" (30 x 16 x 15cm)

Below:
The Love Can (Eva Thomas, photographed by Eva Thomas) 8" x 7" (15 x 17cm)

Linzi Upton

Quilted Yurt

A yurt or ger is a circular trellis-framed tent used as a temporary dwelling by nomadic people living in Central Asia. It is portable yet sturdy and can withstand the harsh winds of the plains. The effective design of a yurt has remained the same for around 2,500 years; collapsible yurts were used by the armies of Genghis Khan in the 12th century.

A yurt is easy to erect, weatherproof, and secure with its lockable wooden doors. Since it is circular and has a low roof, it is easy to keep warm with a wood- or dung-burning stove with a pipe poking out of the central crown. The traditional covering for a yurt is made from felt by rolling out fleeces behind horses or camels. This insulating water-repellent material and the yurt's streamlined shape helps keep out wind.

A yurt is a self-supporting structure that is not anchored to the ground. It is held in place by gravity and opposing forces that give the frame its rigidity when the tension band is tightened around the top of the trellis. Leather thongs, rivets or cords are used to connect the trellis struts so that the walls can be collapsed for storage or expanded when under construction.

The 18ft (5.4m) diameter **Quilted Yurt** has two trellises that are lashed together at the back opposite the doors. The door frame is drilled with holes for cords that hold the trellises in place at the front. Thirty-six 8ft (2.4m) long roof spars are spaced around the trellis walls and each one is held in place with a loop of cord. These spars all fit into holes drilled around the circular roof crown and radiate like the spokes of a wheel. Double wooden doors simply hang on gate brackets attached to the door frame.

The frame can easily be erected in one hour if a small team of helpers is available. The trickiest part of the construction is ensuring that two strong people standing on a step ladder hold the crown aloft centrally until four roof spars are positioned securely.

I was invited to exhibit a collection of quilts at Loch Lomond Quilt Show in 2010. I decided upon the unusual challenge of creating a large quilted yurt. This was inspired by considering the idea of insulating my canvas garden yurt retreat with something functional like duvets, yet more colorful, such as quilted wall hangings. The panels are meant to be viewed from the outside; the intricate quilting on the reverse can be appreciated from inside the yurt.

This project grew into an international collaborative effort involving "stunt" quilters who volunteered to help complete the huge exhibition on time. A selection of fabric was cut, dyed and posted; then stunt quilters worked on tops or quilted panels that were sent back to Scotland. A massive tweed roof using approximately 87yd (80m) of fabric was quilted to look like the corrugated iron that is used on many Scottish farm buildings. Yards of bunting flags were sewn to decorate the inside of the yurt.

The fabric walls of the yurt comprise 18 quilted panels each measuring 30" x 54" (76 by 137cm). These are attached by Velcro to a series of tweed strips that are threaded on to a rope encircling the trellis. This simple hanging method allows the panels to be hung randomly so that every time the yurt is exhibited the walls appear to be differently arranged. Additional panels can be displayed inside.

Below:
Quilted Yurt, framework (Linzi Upton, photographed by Linzi Upton)
96" x 108" (240 x 270cm)

Above:
Quilted Yurt (Linzi Upton,
photographed by Linzi Upton)
96" x 108" (240 x 270cm)

Left:
Quilted Yurt, inside crown
(Linzi Upton, photographed
by Linzi Upton)
96" x 108" (240 x 270cm)

Studio 21

Studio 21 is a group of textile artists who bring together a creative and innovative mix of media and stitched textiles. Formed in 1997, some of the group members share their three-dimensional explorations involving stitched layers presented in innovative and inspirational ways. A full range of the group's work can be seen at their website: studio21textileart.co.uk.

Susan Chapman

I have concerns about the potential isolation and the lack of personal communication that technology has brought; our handwriting is unique to us and as such acts as a metaphor for each person. The panels that make up the piece *Conversation* (left) contain texts of handwriting taken from a lifelong collection of postcards; they are hung in layers, giving a feeling of being able to look into time, with, of course, the obvious reference to reading through the pages of a book. The intention is for the whole piece to describe and own the space it inhabits.

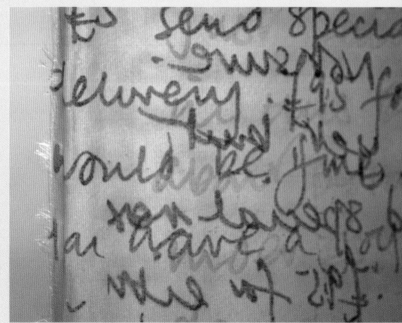

Jill Flower

The majority of my past work is three-dimensional, originating from my love of making practical objects and flamboyant theatrical items. This piece of work, *Home Sweet Home*, was inspired by the world of interior design and the public's love of decorating homes to create place of pleasure, safety, solace, and comfort.

Magazines are deconstructed, reconstructed, stitched, and washed, exposing designer captions and words. Edges are embellished with delicate detailing, forming a large textural book not dissimilar to a collection of fabrics that might be found in interior showrooms. Each page has a different pattern and manipulation, which created a challenge to produce a pleasing composition on both the facing page and the reverse, while maintaining an illusion of a fabric. The pages were worked individually, built up and placed together in many different placements. The whole book is decorated and constructed formally and traditionally, which resulted in a fully working item.

The three-dimensional appearance draws the viewer in to take a closer look, to touch and turn the pages, as if searching for that special texture, fabric or paper, which would transform the home into a very personal and individual sense of place.

Far left and left:
Conversation, whole piece and detail (Susan Chapman, photographed by Susan Chapman) 24" x 144" x 96" (60 x 375 x 250cm)

Above and right:
Home Sweet Home, detail (Jill Flower, photographed by Jill Flower) 22" x 12" x 10½" (56 x 30 x 27cm)

Marion Glover

I am struck by the fantastic tree images represented in Byzantine mosaic ceilings – weird and wonderful shapes, which are unmistakably images of trees. There are trunks and branches with flowers and leaves and fruits equally unusually formed. I have also made a study of early herbal scrolls in the British Library and, fascinated with their liveliness, I filled a sketchbook with details of tree illustrations and my own imagined *Fantasy Trees* (see left).

After experimenting with dyeing fabrics and screen printing, it seemed that the trees needed to come off the page, to come alive in true three-dimensional form. I made a series of maquettes, each larger than the one before and each becoming slightly more unrealistic, but nevertheless tree forms. I used a variety of different weight fabrics, experimented with stiffeners and plasticizers, and a selection of wires and boning. I selected a combination of buckram and strong wire to enable my trees to stand tall and hold their own weight.

The pattern shapes were cut from both buckram and dyed fabric, formed to my designs, wired, stitched, and manipulated to ensure they were able to support themselves vertically. Additional fruits were added later. I created a small forest of trees, each with their own personality and magical liveliness. This work led me on to other three-dimensional textiles and it has given me huge pleasure seeing work take on a vibrant presence of its own.

Above:
3 Fantasy Trees (Marion Glover)
31—12" x 11—4"
(80—30 x 27—15cm)

Below:
Coral Ball (Sam Harvey)
4" (10cm)

Sam Harvey

The quirky creatures found in the sea, in particular coral gardens, are currently the major inspiration for my work. Drawing and collaging is an important part of my research and artistic practice, but the main focus is in stitching sculptures with textiles and found objects. It just feels right for me to "sculpt" with stitched textiles.

The pieces are constructed with ordinary materials – often recycled. The tactile act of creating is very important and the pieces are informed by my drawing, but come together intuitively. Although the origin of the materials is not always obvious, they are selected for their inherent qualities and need to hold their form as three-dimensional objects without reliance on stiffeners or wiring, which is not sympathetic to the texture and aesthetic of the piece.

The base of most of the sculptures is cotton string and usually contains a small solid element – such as a washer, bottle top, or wire, which helps keep the shape – but apart from this the structure must balance on its own.

The embellishments use a range of techniques – led by the required aesthetic and media. Monofilament allows the fronds to maintain a shape yet allows the shape to grow as the elements are stitched together. The pins used in *Coral Ball* provide a dramatic, rigid look.

Debbie Lyddon

Auricle

Auricle, detail (Debbie Lyddon, photographed by C. June Barnes) 78" x 16" x 8" (200 x 40 x 20cm) Made from linen, paraffin wax, shoe polish and wire

Auricle comes from a series of work – *Gestural Lines* – that explores how the sounds within our environment can be described visually. This concept is explored by considering how we would describe abstract sound with gestures, using our hands and bodies: how would we draw sound in the air and what shapes do our hands and bodies make when trying to re-describe sound? The resulting gestural marks occur in space, therefore their re-description is in three-dimensional form.

The dimension and form of *Auricle* are within reach of my outstretched arms. Layers of marks – both two-dimensional and three-dimensional – are built up to produce a simple but evocative series of cloth works aimed to stimulate the sense of touch. The rhythmical impetus of the repeated vertical line suggests the qualities of sound.

Far left and left:
Floe Edge 1 and 2, with detail
(Sandra Meech, photographed by
Sandra Meech)
16" x 70" x 3" (40 x 180 x 7cm)

Sandra Meech

Ice, in all forms, is a passion with me, as testified by my collection of
photographs accumulated over the years. From the Canadian Arctic and
the Rockies, to Iceland, the majesty and immensity of glaciers has always
fascinated me; the ebb and flow of the layers, the crystalline beauty of the
turquoise edge and the evidence of history within. Aerial views of ocean ice
in spring add to the pattern and texture that could eventually be included
in my own textile work.

Sketchbooks and paper collage composition is the way I begin. It
consolidates ideas and gives me time to think and plan a way forward.
Drawing marks on a page will inform stitch; painted and torn paper
could suggest texture and dimension.

Photographs play a major part in my work and images are transferred
two ways – with an acrylic medium or inkjet heat transfer papers. Adding
painted or printed cloth to the fabric collage can give a lively and more
energetic surface. For these slice of quilt-art pieces, I have used metal wire-
form to manipulate the surface, adding dimension with copper
and orange and copper thread to suggest melting ice.

As I read more and more in the news about global warming and see
evidence around the world, I know it will be a subject that will fill me with
inspiration for years to come.

Mary Morris

My work is concerned with the way we view landscape and how this is affected by memory. The layers of physical marks and residual traces of lives lived in a landscape combine with memory and understanding to make a complex composite perception of place. *Profusion* (right) is my contribution to Studio 21's collaborative project *Continuum: A Sense of Place*. The sense of place I am concerned with here is not so much a single geographical location but more a point in time – an accumulation of fragmentary recollections and traces of the past. The physical box-like units in a grid form create an organizing structure, or a way of containing and rationalizing – making order and sense. Some units within the grid are open and clearly visible, while others conceal and protect their contents within wrapped bundles. I use a variety of media including oil, encaustic wax, pigment, photography, and cloth.

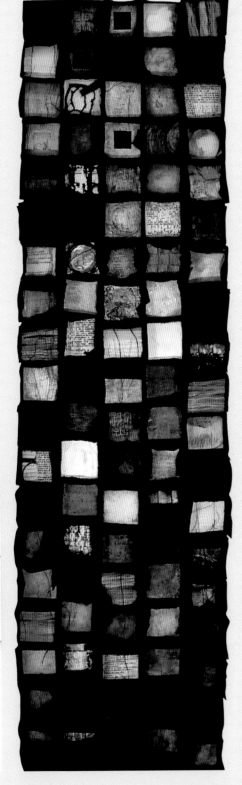

Far right and right:
Profusion, detail (Mary Morris)
22" x 78" x 4" (56 x 200 x 10cm)

Dawn Thorne

I am inspired by architecture, structure, form, and the rhythmic associations of a repeated unit. Adding into the equation the principles of physics that a form occupies and impacts upon its surroundings within a given space has pushed me in the dimensional direction.

I have found that working in three dimensions gives me a hands-on connection with my textiles. Manipulating and handling machine-constructed textiles is very satisfying. Interesting shapes and layers sometimes evolve spontaneously and rhythmically. Working in this way has enabled me to expand my textile art practice through the use of both hard and soft materials, the properties of which allow me to obtain the depth of imagery I want through the use of transparency and the desire to achieve illusion.

I like to create pieces that can be viewed from all angles and which can be walked around and engaged with. My choice to work with hard acrylic sheet as a working fabric has evolved from the need to be able to create reflections and cast shadows within my design ideas as well as providing the structure. Challenges faced when I started out using this hard plastic were resolved by hours of playing and finding out how far I could fabricate the material using limited resources in the comfort of a low-tech home studio without the use of expensive equipment. I soon discovered through experimentation that acrylic can be drilled, bent, stitched, printed, and etched, offering a wealth of possibilities.

Whether incorporating hard materials or just using soft or constructed stitched textiles I do find that, even when I have to work to a two-dimensional brief, I automatically find I am manipulating the surface into undulating folds or creating relief in some way or another.

Appendix

The following instructions are for drawing some of the basic shapes required for the patterns used in a few of the exercises in the book. Although there are other methods I have found these to be the most straightforward.

Equilateral Triangle (three equal sides)

Refer to the diagram on page 70.

1 Start with a base line A–B.
2 Mark an inside angle of 60° at each end of the base line A–B.
3 Draw a line from A along the 60° line extending it beyond the length of the base line.
4 Draw a line from B along the 60° line extending it beyond the length of the base line.
5 These two lines will meet at C.
6 Line A–C and B–C will equal A–B.

Smaller equilateral triangles can be drawn using a pair of compasses set with a radius equal to A–B and using A and B as the centers of arcs that intersect at C.

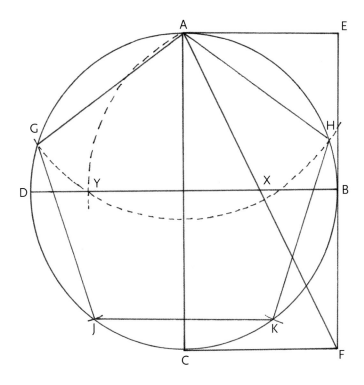

Regular Pentagon
(five equal sides)

1 Draw a circle and mark the diameters at A, B, C and D.
2 In one semicircle draw the rectangle A–E–F–C with the ratio 2:1 (i.e. the height twice the width).
3 Draw the diagonal A–F and mark the point X where A–F and B–D intersect.
4 With center X and radius X–A draw an arc through Y.
5 With center A and radius A–Y draw an arc that intersects the circle at G and H.
6 With centers G and H and the same radius A–Y, make two more arcs cutting the circle at J and K.
7 Draw the pentagon A–H–K–J–G–A.

Alternative way to draw a regular pentagon (five equal sides with internal angles of 108°):

1 Start with a line A–B.
2 Mark an angle of 108° outwards from point B.
3 Mark a point C the same length as the base line along this angle – B–C.
4 Repeat steps 2 and 3 from the new points, establishing lines C–D, D–E, and F–A.

Oval or Ellipse

1 Draw two concentric circles, one with the diameter equal to the major axis (A–B) of the ellipse required and the other with a diameter equal to the diameter of the minor axis (C–D).
2 Draw diagonals across the circles. You need only draw a few diameters across the circle but you will draw a more accurate ellipse with more. In the illustration, radiating lines of 30° were used.
3 Draw a horizontal line outwards at each intersection of the minor circle with this grid.
4 Draw a vertical line inwards at each intersection of the major circle with this grid.
5 Mark the intersecting points of these vertical and horizontal lines.
6 Join these points up (as in dotted line A–C) with a smoothly curving line to draw the perimeter of the ellipse.
7 Adding extra lines close to the major axis will help you to get a smoother curve or ellipse.

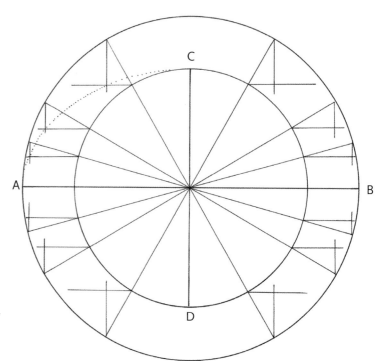

Regular Hexagon
(six equal sides with internal angles of 120°)

Refer to the diagram on page 89.

1 Start with a line AB.
2 Mark an angle of 120° outwards from point B.
3 Mark a point C the same length as the base line along this angle – B–C.
4 Repeat steps 2 and 3 establishing lines C–D, D–E, E–F and F–A.

Hexagon constructed using the *vesica piscis*

Draw **vesica piscis** using a circle with center A. Draw a second circle with the same radius using a point B on the circumference of the first circle as its center. Mark the two points of intersection C and D, creating the **vesica** A–B–C–D.

1 Draw an arc with C as the center, with radius C–B, the same as the first two circles. This arc cuts the second circle at E.
2 Repeat step 1 using D as the center with the radius B–D. Mark the intersection of this arc and the second circle F.
3 Repeat using either E or F as the center of the arc to find point G on the second circle. G also lies on the extended line A–B where it intersects the circumference of the second circle.
4 Draw the hexagon A–C–E–G–F–D–A.
5 Note that two equilateral triangles are formed within the **vesica** – A–B–C and A–B–D.

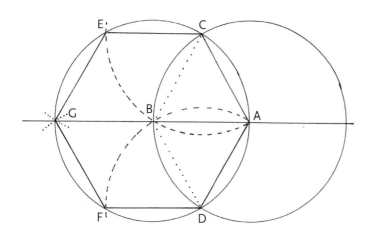

Suppliers

United Kingdom

Art Van Go
The Studios
1 Stevenage Road
Knebworth
Hertfordshire SG3 6AN
artvango.co.uk
*Wide range of art supplies –
Markal (Shiva) Paintstiks*

Barnyarns (Ripon) Ltd
Canal Wharf
Bondgate Green
Ripon
North Yorkshire HG4 1AQ
barnyarns.co.uk
superiorthreads.co.uk
Water soluble thread

Kemtex Educational Supplies
Chorley Business & Technology Centre
Euxton Lane
Chorley
Lancashire PR7 6TE
kemtex.co.uk
Dyestuffs and chemicals

MacCulloch & Wallis
25–26 Dering Street
London W1S 1AT
maccullough-wallis.co.uk
Boning and milliners' wire

Naish Felts Ltd
Crow Lane
Wilton, Salisbury
Wiltshire SP2 0HD
naishfelts.co.uk
*Viscose wool felt – including
colored. Avoid white*

Rainbow Silks
6 Wheelers Yard
High Street
Great Missenden
Bucks HP16 0AL
rainbowsilks.co.uk
Lamitex, Pellon, silk fabric

Ready Made Canvas
11 Garman Road
London N17 0UR
readymadecanvas.com
Wide range of stretched canvas sizes

The Silk Route
Cross Cottage
Cross Lane
Frimley Green
Surrey GU16 6LN
thesilkroute.co.uk
Wide range of silk fabric

Whaleys (Bradford) Ltd
Harris Court
Great Horton
Bradford
West Yorkshire BD7 4EQ
whaleys-bradford.ltd.uk
*Wide range of natural fiber fabrics;
viscose-wool felt but specify that it is for
shrinkage – you do not want the white,
bleached product, which doesn't shrink
as effectively*

USA

Dharma Trading Co
1604 Fourth St.
San Rafael CA 94901
dharmtrading.com
Dyes, fabric, chemicals, advice

PRO Chemical & Dye
P.O. Box 14
Somerset MA 02726
prochemical.com
Dyes, chemicals

Glossary

Backing: the layer of fabric on the back of a quilt.

Batting: the soft material used as a stuffing between the quilt top and quilt backing.

Bias: the grain of woven fabric that is at a 45° angle to the selvages.

Concave: an edge or outline that curves inwards.

Congruent: two figures are congruent if they have the same shape and size.

Convex: an edge or outline that curves outwards.

Cording: soft cords such as knitting cotton can be stitched to the underside of fabric using a twin needle. Some machines have an extra hole in the stitch plate to thread the cord through to guide it. Others use a special attachment fitted to the stitch plate. Use a twin needle (you will need two threads on top) and select a cord that passes through the cording hole or guide comfortably, and that runs smoothly between the twin needles. Thread the cord through the hole or guide and pull it to the back of the machine, laying it under the pressure foot. As you stitch, the cord will automatically lie directly in between the two lines of stitching and be secured to the underside of the fabric with the bobbin thread. If your machine doesn't have either of these facilities, a piece of drinking straw taped on to the machine bed in front of the needle works well. This also enables the use of cords too thick to go through the hole or guide – the twin needle used must be wide enough to accommodate the thicker cord.

Couched: a thread is laid down on the surface of the work and stitched in place with another thread, using either small stitches worked over the top by hand, or a zigzag stitch if worked by machine.

Ellipse: a circle flattened in one direction creates an ellipse, or an oval shape. It has two axes – the longer major axis and the shorter minor axis.

Embellishment: decorative stitches or items that are added to a quilt, including buttons, beads, embroidery or other thread.

Feed dog: the mechanical teeth under the presser foot area of a sewing machine, which move to pull the fabric through the machine. For free-motion quilting or embroidery or needle darning the feed dog is lowered or covered.

Foundation piecing: a method of sewing fabric pieces on the reverse side of a paper pattern or foundation fabric. Log-cabin blocks can also be stitched on to a foundation piece of batting from the front of the work. (The blocks for *Jewel Boxes* on page 68 were stitched from the back with the pattern drawn on to papers.)

Free machine stitch: stitching with the feed dog dropped or covered, making it necessary to move the fabric in order to form stitches. This enables the operator to move the fabric around in all directions, stitching free-form patterns and shapes without turning the work around.

Grain: the lengthwise and crosswise threads of a woven fabric. A grain-line arrow, printed on a pattern, helps you properly place your quilt pattern piece on the fabric.

Log cabin: a quilt pattern in which narrow fabric strips, or logs, surround a center square to form a block.

Perimeter: a path that surrounds an area. From the Greek *peri* (around) and **meter** (measure). The term may be used either for the path or the length of the outline of a shape. The perimeter of a circular area is called the circumference.

Polyhedron: a geometric solid in three dimensions with flat faces and straight edges.

Registration marks: a dressmaking term relating to the marks on a pattern, which indicate what points on a seam must match.

Sandwich: The top, middle, and back layers of a quilt.

Satin stitch: a tightly packed (no spaces showing through of the fabric) zigzag stitch.

Seam allowance: the margin of fabric between the seam and the raw edge. The quilting seam allowance is ¼" (6mm).

Sewer's Aid: a silicone-based product, which, when added to thread by running a bead along the surface of the reel, helps the thread run through the tension discs and needle more smoothly. Helps to minimize thread shredding.

Stay stitching: a dressmaking term describing a single line of stitching, which helps to stabilise the fabric, preventing it from becoming stretched or distorted. Stay stitching in dressmaking is usually called for on the edge of a piece of fabric that has a bias cut to it, which would allow the fabric easily to become distorted. It serves the same purpose when piecing geometric shapes to one another.

Thread weight: the cotton count system (50, 60 etc.) refers to the number of 840yd hanks of yarn it takes to weigh 1lb – the more hanks the thinner the thread. A 30 weight thread is therefore thicker than a 50.

Trapunto: a method of quilting with at least two layers; shapes are quilted and padded traditionally from the underside through a slit or more recently by adding an extra layer of batting to the underside of the top layer in the desired pattern areas before layering, thus producing a raised surface on the quilt.

Water-soluble pen: a chemical-based pen used to add a temporary mark on fabric. To avoid future unwanted marking the chemical needs to be totally removed with cold water when the work is complete; just sponging off is not sufficient. There is also available a similar marking pen, which loses pigment through the moisture in the air. Even though the color is no longer there the chemical is and also needs removing with cold water – the chemical may turn into brown marks on the fabric if exposed to heat and light later, so it is better to be safe than sorry.

Water-soluble thread: a thread used temporarily to hold layers or items in place. It dissolves when washed. Perfect for machine trapunto.

Wulff net or grid: a special graph paper that maps stereographic projection, which projects a sphere on to a plane. It is also called a stereonet.

Zigzag stitch: a side-to-side stitch that can be used for machine appliqué. It can be shortened and closely spaced so it looks like a satin stitch.

Recommended Reading

Dimension and Inspiration

Agkathidis, Asterios, *Modular Structures*. Book Industry Services (BIS), 2009.

Avella, Natalie, *Paper Engineering*. Rotovision, 2009.

Critchlow, Keith, *The Hidden Geometry of Flowers*. Floris Books, 2011.

Genders, Carolyn, *Pattern, Colour and Form*. A&C Black, 2009.

Gjerde, Eric, *Origami Tessellations*. CRC Press, 2009.

Hardy, Madeline and Kesseler, Rob, *Pollen: The Hidden Sexuality of Flowers*. Papadakis, 2009.

Herriott, Luke, *The Packaging and Design Templates Sourcebook*.

Jackson, Paul, *Folding Techniques for Designers*. Laurence King, 2011.

La Plantz, Dhereen, *Cover to Cover*. Lark Books, 1999.

Lawlor, Robert, *Sacred Geometry*. Thames & Hudson, 2007.

Lim, Joseph, *Bio-Structural Analogies in Architecture*. BIS Publishers, 2009.

Maurer-Mathison, Diane, *Paper in Three Dimensions*. Watson-Guptill Publications, 2006.

Nakano, Dokuohtei, *Easy Origami*. Dover Publications, 2000.

Olden, Scott, *Golden Section*. Wooden Books, 2006.

Scott, Jac, *Textile Perspectives in Mixed-Media Sculpture*. Crowood Press, 2003.

Sharp, John, *D-Forms*. Tarquin, 2009.

Smith, A.G., *Cut and Assemble 3-D Geometrical Shapes*. Dover Publications, 2003.

Smith, Maggie, *Get Plastered*. Roundtuit Publishing, 2008.

Stuppy, Wolfgang and Kesseler, Rob, *The Bizarre and Incredible World of Plants*. Papadakis, 2009.

Stuppy, Wolfgang and Kesseler, Rob, *Seeds – Time Capsules of Life*. Papadakis, 2009.

Sutton, Andrew, *Ruler and Compass – Practical Geometric Constructions*. Wooden Books, 2009.

Sutton, Daud, *Platonic and Archimedean Solids*. Wooden Books, 2005.

Vyzoviti, Sophia, *Folding Architecture*. BIS Publishers, 2004.

Vyzoviti, Sophia, *Supersurfaces*. BIS Publishers, 2006.

The Penland Book of Handmade Books.

Stitch and Design

Barnes, C June. *Stitching to Dye in Quilt Art*. Batsford, 2008.

Edmonds, Janet. *Three-dimensional Embroidery*. Batsford, 2005.

Grey, Maggie. *Raising the Surface with Machine Embroidery*. Batsford, 2003.

Meech, Sandra. *Contemporary Quilts, Design, Surface and Stitch*. Batsford, 2003.

Dyeing

Dunnewold, Jane, *Complex Cloth: A Comprehensive Guide to Surface Design*. Martingale & Company, 1996.

Dunnewold, Jane, *Art Cloth: A Guide to Surface Design for Fabric*. Interweave Press Inc, 2010.

Johnston, Ann, *Color by Accident*. Ann Johnston, 1997.

Johnston, Ann, *Color by Design*. Ann Johnston, 2001.

Morgan, Leslie, *Tray Dyeing*. Committed to Cloth, 2007.

Index